The

PARAPROFESSIONAL'S
Essential Guide to
Inclusive Education

THIRD EDITION

The PARAPROFESSIONAL'S Essential Guide to Inclusive Education

THIRD EDITION

PEGGY A. HAMMEKEN

CORWIN PRESS
A SAGE Company

For information:

Corwin Press
A SAGE Company
2455 Teller Road
Thousand Oaks, California 91320
www.corwinpress.com

SAGE Ltd.
1 Oliver's Yard
55 City Road
London EC1Y 1SP
United Kingdom

SAGE India Pvt. Ltd.
B 1/I 1 Mohan Cooperative
   Industrial Area
Mathura Road, New Delhi
India

SAGE Asia-Pacific Pte. Ltd.
33 Pekin Street #02-01
Far East Square
Singapore 048763

Printed in the United States of America.

Library of Congress Cataloging-in-Publication Data

Hammeken, Peggy A.
The paraprofessional's essential guide to inclusive education / Peggy A. Hammeken.—3rd ed.
    p. cm.
Rev. ed. of: Inclusion: an essential guide for the paraprofessional. c2003.
Includes bibliographical references and index.
ISBN 978-1-4129-6610-8 (hardcover w/cd)—ISBN 978-1-4129-6611-5 (pbk. w/cd)

    1. Children with disabilities—Education—United States—Handbooks, manuals, etc. 2. Inclusive education—United States—Handbooks, manuals, etc. 3. Teachers' assistants—United States—Handbooks, manuals, etc. 4. Special education—Planning—Handbooks, manuals, etc. I. Hammeken, Peggy A. Inclusion. II. Title.

LC4031.H34 2009
371.90973—dc22   2008034486

This book is printed on acid-free paper.

        11   12   10   9   8   7   6   5   4   3   2

Acquisitions Editor:	David Chao
Associate Editor:	Megan Bedell
Production Editor:	Cassandra Margaret Seibel
Copy Editor:	Sarah J. Duffy
Typesetter:	C&M Digitals (P) Ltd.
Proofreader:	Jenifer Kooiman
Indexer:	Terri Corry
Cover Designer:	Michael Dubowe

Contents

Preface

Every job is a self-portrait of the person who did it.
Autograph your work with excellence.

Unknown

Paraprofessionals are valuable, essential (and often overlooked) members of the special education team. Without the support of these hardworking people, a well-organized and successful inclusive education program is difficult if not impossible to implement. Yet there are few publications developed specifically as hands-on working manuals for the paraprofessional.

As a special educator, I was involved in the implementation and set-up of inclusive programs. The first book I wrote, in 1995, was a manual for educators titled *Inclusion: 450 Strategies for Success.* At the time, inclusive education was in its infancy, and the number of paraprofessionals working in special education was limited. As inclusive education evolved, the number of paraprofessionals has increased dramatically. I was fortunate to be involved with many exceptional paraprofessionals, working alongside and with them in inservice training. I compiled ideas and asked simple questions such as "What support do you need to make your job easier?" and "What tools will help you be successful?" The first edition of this book, *Inclusion: An Essential Guide for the Paraprofessional*, also published in 1996, evolved from these conversations. Now in its third edition, it bears little resemblance to the first edition. Since that time, many changes have occurred in special education, and this publication has evolved along with the system.

The purpose of this book is to be a concrete resource for paraprofessionals to use daily. It answers common questions, provides extensive strategies to help students in all areas of the curriculum, and incorporates a collection of forms and templates to support paraprofessionals and students. Although the primary audience is paraprofessionals, earlier editions of this book have been widely used as a training tool by educators and staff development professionals. It is also a helpful resource for parents to differentiate the roles of both educators and paraprofessionals in relation to their children's educational program.

Whether you are experienced, newly hired, or simply exploring the field of special education as a possible career change, this book is for you. The special education field is complex and operates within a due process system established by governing laws. To work in this field, it is important to understand the system and the students with whom you will work. With a strong knowledge base, you will be prepared, confident, and comfortable working with this special population of students. Their needs determine the role and responsibilities for each paraprofessional; therefore, your job description may be completely different from that of your colleagues. Often there is a misconception that special education is a "place," but in reality it is a set of services provided to students, and the services fluctuate depending on the unique needs of each student.

ABOUT THIS BOOK

The Paraprofessional's Essential Guide to Inclusive Education, Third Edition, is a practical hands-on resource for use in the classroom or resource room setting. Although the focus is students with special needs, many of the strategies are appropriate for general education students who are struggling in school and may need additional support to experience success.

The hundreds of numbered strategies in this publication are divided by topic. The numbering system is intended to help you document your use of the strategies along with your results. It simplifies record keeping and supports the documentation of student progress. With hundreds of easy-to-implement ideas at your fingertips, this book will make your job easier. Throughout the text, I discuss forms that can help with communication, planning, documentation, supplemental student aids, and more. All of these forms can be found in the Resources.

What's New in This Edition

Some of the highlights of this completely revised third edition include a new chapter on reading (Chapter 10), new sections within existing chapters, additional activities for individual or inservice use, and approximately 80 new strategies and 12 new forms (which are available on CD-ROM for easy reproduction).

Chapter 10 is dedicated to helping struggling readers in the classroom. It offers specific strategies and materials to enhance student support in the areas of reading decoding, comprehension, and vocabulary development, and it provides new supplemental forms. Another major change is the revision of Chapter 7, "Accommodations and Modifications," which now clearly distinguishes between these two areas in terms of environment as well as program planning. After reading Chapter 7, you will clearly understand and easily distinguish between these frequently confused areas. Educators and paraprofessionals have indicated the usefulness of the previous edition's activities and hypothetical situations, which are used to develop a skill, to increase understanding of situations that may occur, or as an inservice tool. Therefore, additional activities have been included in this edition. Of course, no book is complete without including the current updates to federal legislation. Therefore, revisions include an update to disability areas in the law and a section discussing possible classroom implications.

So whether you are about to pursue your first job, have recently been hired by a school system, or are an experienced paraprofessional, this book will provide the support needed to make your job a little easier.

Committing your career to inclusive schooling and supporting students with special needs in the classroom is both challenging and rewarding. With your support, students will develop not only academically but also socially and emotionally to reach their full potential. You will make a difference in the lives of many children!

Peggy Hammeken

Acknowledgments

Corwin Press gratefully acknowledges the contributions of the following reviewers:

Renee Bernhardt, Special Education Teacher
Johnston Elementary School, Woodstock, GA

Dawne Dragonetti, Special Education Teacher and Instructional Coach
Center School, Stow, MA

Esther Eacho, Learning Disabilities Resource Teacher
Aldrin Elementary School, Reston, VA

Beverly Plagge, Paraprofessional Educator
Area Education Agency, Latimer, IA

About the Author

Peggy A. Hammeken began her career as an elementary teacher at the American Embassy School in Mexico City. Upon returning to the United States, she taught students in the areas of specific learning disabilities, mental retardation, and emotional/behavior disorders. With the implementation of inclusive education, she was involved in setting up inclusive programs and staff development and training for educators and paraprofessionals, and she has authored three books on the subject. Ms. Hammeken received her bachelor's degree in elementary teaching and her master's degree in special education from Minnesota State University, Mankato, and founded Peytral Publications, a publishing house focusing on inclusive education of students.

Introduction

If you think you're too small to make a difference, you obviously
have never been in bed with a mosquito!

Michele Walker

The educational institution is an ever-evolving entity, and few areas have experienced more change in recent history than the field of special education. Prior to 1975, the standards for educating students with disabilities varied greatly on a national scale. The majority of students with special needs received their education in segregated classrooms and specialized schools. It was not atypical for students with severe disabilities to be placed into institutions and receive no formal education.

The most important legal change for students with disabilities occurred in 1975 with passage of the Education for All Handicapped Children Act, which required the educational system to face the challenge of including all students with disabilities in the general education setting. The law guaranteed a "free, appropriate public education" for every student and mandated that all children with disabilities be educated with their peers to the "maximum extent appropriate" in the "least restrictive environment." In 1997 this law was amended as the Individuals with Disabilities Education Act (IDEA-97), commonly referred to as IDEA. This update significantly changed the interaction of the regular and special education systems by combining them into a single system. In November 2004, IDEA was again reauthorized, this time as the Individual with Disabilities Education Improvement Act (IDEIA). The inclusive settings of today evolved and developed from this law.

More recently, the U.S. Congress added new provisions to federal education law with the No Child Left Behind Act of 2001 (NCLB), which increases the standards of accountability for states, school districts, and schools and enacts the theories of standards-based education reform, formerly known as outcome-based education. NCLB mandates that states develop assessments of basic skills, assessments that are required for all students at various grade levels throughout their educational career. Although this law is not specifically a special education initiative, special education students are required to take the assessments.

Both NCLB and IDEIA refer to the use of scientific, research-based strategies to monitor student achievement. Previous to the implementation of IDEIA, student placement in special education relied on a significant discrepancy between a student's IQ score and achievement in the classroom. IDEIA removed this requirement and required that states permit districts to adopt alternative models, including the response to intervention (RTI) model, a multistep approach to providing services and interventions to students who struggle with learning at increasing levels of intensity. Careful monitoring of student progress is documented at each stage of the intervention. The resulting data provides the basis to make decisions about the need for further research-based instruction and/or intervention in general education, special education, or both. Researchers suggest that one of the benefits of RTI is that it merges special education into the overall policies of NCLB with clear standards and useful measurement and it lays the groundwork for enhancing the performance of all students. The RTI process has the potential to limit the amount of academic failure that any student experiences and to increase the accuracy of special education evaluations. It may reduce the number of students who are mistakenly identified as having learning disabilities when actually their learning problems are due to, for example, cultural differences or the lack of adequate instruction. Information and data gathered by the RTI process can lead to earlier identification of children with true disabilities and at an earlier age.

To provide support and meet the needs of students in the general education setting, the legislation empowers school districts to hire the necessary personnel. IDEIA also stipulates that districts must establish and maintain standards to assure that all personnel receive adequate training and supervision. Without the support of paraprofessionals, it is very difficult, if not impossible, to include and meet the needs of special education students in the general education environment.

School districts across the country continue to struggle with inclusive education and the requirements necessary to comply with federal guidelines. And with the implementation of inclusive education, educators are required to expand their roles. Teaching is no longer one educator leading a homogeneous group of students. Today's typical classroom often includes a general education teacher, a special education teacher, paraprofessionals, and consultants working collaboratively to meet the needs of all students. With a wide array of students—students with special needs, students who are gifted and talented, students whose native language is not English, to name only a few—this is a daunting task. All of these students need additional support in the classroom environment to obtain the best education possible.

With the inclusive education movement, the creation of new jobs for paraprofessionals has increased dramatically. In fact, the need for qualified paraprofessionals continues to rise with the implementation of NCLB and RTI. The National Center on Educational Statistics (NCES; 2000) reported a 48 percent increase in instructional paraprofessional employment between 1990 and 1998, compared to only a 13 percent increase in student enrollment and an 18 percent increase in teacher employment. During the 2003–2004 school year, NCES reported that 91 percent of public schools employed instructional paraprofessionals, with an average of eight full-time paraprofessionals per school.

Nationwide, school districts are in various stages of hiring and training paraprofessionals. In newly implemented programs, recently hired paraprofessionals with little or no formal training are often expected to work with students immediately. School districts with inclusive programs in place frequently have extensive training programs, and training often occurs before paraprofessionals begin to work with students. Whether you are a newly hired or experienced paraprofessional, this book provides an abundance of ideas and information to help you when working in the inclusive setting.

Building Background

The only person who loves a change is a wet baby.

Ray Blitzer

What differentiates the typical inclusive classroom of today from the traditional mainstream classroom of the past? Today's inclusive classroom includes all students, with and without disabilities. Previously, students with special needs were included in the classroom only when they were able to participate fully in the class activity. Therefore, students with special needs participated in nonacademic activities such as music, physical education, free time, and lunch. Most instruction occurred in segregated rooms, and all students with special needs received the same classroom placement, no matter what the handicapping condition. They were usually classified as "yours" or "mine" but rarely as "ours." These students reentered classrooms when they reached their academic goals. For example, a student with a three-year discrepancy in the area of reading received a supplemental curriculum in the hopes of closing the achievement gap and "catching up" to the other students in the class. Once the acceptable level of proficiency was achieved, the student was "permitted" to return to the mainstream classroom. For some students, supplemental remediation was sufficient and they "earned" the right to return to the classroom, but for many the gap widened, which resulted in special classes for their entire academic career.

In today's inclusive environments, it is common to see students with and without disabilities playing together, working on projects collaboratively, and supporting one another. All students are an integral part of the classroom community. Upon close observation of today's classroom environment, it becomes apparent that some students are completing assignments and carrying out activities that are entirely different from the activities of their peers. The majority of students may be working on a written language assignment at their desks, while others may be completing the assignment on the computer or dictating their response to a scribe. During reading, it is rare to see all students with their textbooks open, reading independently and in silence. One student may be seated with a partner, listening to the material as the partner reads it out loud. Another student may be seated in front of a computer listening as the computer reads the text. A small group of students may be seated with an adult, reading in a round-robin fashion or reading aloud simultaneously. During math class, a small number of students may be using manipulative objects and calculators during a test whereas others are completing the test independently. Some students may have a special computer with programs geared to their specific level. Some students also may be working in collaborative groups, in which each student has a specific responsibility within the group. Today's classroom has definitely changed!

In the inclusive classroom, students may also have separate goals and expected outcomes for various educational activities. During large-group instruction, some students may have a socialization goal instead of an academic goal. In contrast to the conventional classroom of the past, today's inclusive classroom has a completely different setup. Rarely in the inclusive classroom will you see all students carrying out the same assignments at the same time while using the same approach to learning.

ACTIVITIES

Although they are fairly simple in nature, the next two activities can help you understand some of the difficulties that students encounter, both socially and academically, in a dual-education setting.

Activity 1: Inclusion Versus Exclusion

Materials needed: paper and pencil.

To complete this activity, fold the paper in half to create two columns. Label the left column *Inclusion* and the right column *Exclusion*.

Inclusion. What does the word mean? Take a moment to think about an event during your childhood or teenage years when you belonged to a group and felt part of the community. Perhaps you were a member of the band or orchestra, a club, a sports team, or it was a family event. Close your eyes, and step back in time. Think about the event, the people involved, and the feelings associated with the event. Think about how you felt when you participated in or belonged to this group. When you are ready, take a moment to write words in the Inclusion column that describe how you felt when included.

Now think about exclusion. Take a moment to recall a childhood event from which you were excluded. Perhaps it was a bus ride when you sat alone, an activity or party to which you were not invited, or a family event at which a sibling received all the attention. Once again, close your eyes and return to that moment. Think about how you felt. Write words in the Exclusion column that describe how you felt.

Now compare the two word lists. Which is longer? More often than not, the second list pertaining to the exclusion activity is longer. Powerful words such as *lonely, misunderstood, rejected, depressed,* and *unhappy* usually are the first that come to mind. On the other hand, the words associated with the inclusion activity include *content, happy, belonging,* and *accepted.*

As students enter school, there is a strong desire to be accepted by their peers. They want to belong, feel safe, and be part of the school community. Students accepted by their peers and those who feel part of the group are more liable to learn. Students who are comfortable and happy are less likely to be afraid to take the educational risks involved in learning. When students are consistently excluded from classroom activities, it is difficult to make friends, establish a sense of belonging, and feel part of the community.

Activity 2: What Do I Do Now?

Materials needed: paper and pencil.

Imagine that you are taking a class at the university. You arrive late, just as the professor is concluding the lecture. You slide into your seat with the hope that the professor does not notice. On the table is an assignment that you must complete. Because you were not in the class for the lecture or instruction, you have no idea what to do.

As an adult student, you have several choices. You can decide to set up an appointment with the professor to discuss the assignment, perhaps ask colleagues for help, or choose to write a note on the assignment that you arrived late and therefore cannot complete it. As an adult, you are able to make these decisions. And the professor is more likely to be lenient because you are an adult.

Now, let us change the hypothetical situation to involve an elementary-level student. Imagine that John, a sixth-grade student, has encountered a similar situation in his classroom. He returned to his class from the resource room where he receives individual reading instruction in a supplemental reading series. (John is currently reading at a fourth-grade level.) The class finished its reading lesson early, and the English block has started. As John sits down, he glances at the English assignment on his desk. He has no clue how to proceed. He missed the classroom instruction and cannot read or complete the assignment alone. What options are available to John? Take a moment to list as many options as you can think of, and compare the options you listed to the following possibilities:

1. John tries to complete the English assignment without instruction.

2. John sits quietly until a peer or the teacher is available to assist him.

3. John completes an unrelated assignment or project.

4. John begins to talk and disrupts the other students who are working.

In the classroom environment, these situations frequently occur. Upon examination, each option is a difficult situation for John. Let us examine why.

Option 1: John tries to complete the English assignment without instruction.

Students with disabilities often need extra time to complete assignments without appropriate modifications. In this situation, John not only missed the instruction, but also has less time to complete the assignment. He may need support with both reading and writing; therefore, it may be very difficult for him to find the answers in a text or to read another student's notes. It is unlikely that he will be able to complete the assignment on his own.

Option 2: John sits quietly until a peer or the teacher is available to assist him.

John must transition between the resource room and his classroom. During each transition, approximately 10 minutes of actively engaged learning time is lost, including time spent gathering and returning materials in each class. It is also likely that John met a friend in the hallway or stopped by the bathroom, which could easily extend the transition time to 20 minutes. If he returns to the classroom and does not know what to do or how to complete the assignment, he must wait until help arrives. With 25 or more students in the class, the teacher is unable to attend to John immediately.

On a weekly basis, these short time periods can easily amount to over two hours of active learning time. If John leaves the classroom more than once a day, the active learning time (time on task) decreases substantially.

Option 3: John completes an unrelated assignment or project.

This is a frequently used option. John may use the time to complete other class work, assignments, or projects that he can do independently. In this scenario, several assumptions are frequently made by the others in the classroom. Classmates may think that John is not required to complete the same assignments. They often feel that this is unfair. The misconceptions of others may end up having a negative impact on John's self-esteem.

Option 4: John begins to talk and disrupts the other students who are working.

John returns to class with no available support. No appropriate assignment is available, so he begins to talk to or disrupt other students. The teacher reprimands him.

With each of the previous options, there are additional questions to address. If John is required to complete the English assignment, when will he find the time? Will he need to complete the assignment as homework? During recess? If he does not complete this assignment, will he be able to complete the next assignment or is this assignment a prerequisite to the next lesson? With these options, it is very easy to see that John could soon begin to dislike school and lose the desire to learn. Additional homework, staying in during recess, and using free time to catch up are not viable options for an energetic elementary-age boy.

It is very difficult for a student to be successful in the classroom setting while working within a fragmented educational program. In a dual-educational system, it is often the case that students who require the most consistency in programming receive the least. They must manage two curriculums, two classrooms, two (or more) teachers, and, frequently, two sets of rules.

Special education is not a place or a special room. It is a service provided to a group of students. Although the classroom setting is not appropriate for all students with special needs, it is the first option for placement. For some students, simple accommodations help them experience success. For others, modifications and additional support is required. Frequently, paraprofessionals are the people who provide this additional support, and with it the majority of students will learn and flourish in the classroom. With paraprofessionals in the classroom, the students' time on task increases because valuable learning time is no longer lost during transitions. Also, the flexibility of general education teachers increases because they do not have to wait for students to return to the class. Lesson times can be monitored and adjusted immediately, increasing the actively engaged learning time for all students.

INCLUSIVE PRACTICES: MYTH AND REALITY

Inclusive programs are not all the same. There is no blueprint for the development and structure of an inclusive program. They vary among states, districts, schools, and even classrooms in the same building. Federal law provides the framework, and each program is designed around the students' unique needs.

There are many myths related to inclusive education. To help dispel them, let us look at the most common.

Myth: General education students receive a watered-down curriculum to compensate for students with special needs in the classroom.

Reality: The general education curriculum is adapted and modified to meet the specific needs of individual students. Adaptations and modifications may include alternate forms of testing, extra class time to complete assignments, reading materials aloud to students, and adjusting the goals and objectives for individual students. These changes have virtually no impact on the curriculum for the other students.

Myth: All students with disabilities must complete each assignment in the same manner as the students in the general education classroom.

Reality: Each student's needs are determined in an individualized education plan, which is a legal document that lists special accommodations and modifications.

Myth: Students placed in the general education class are expected to achieve without support and assistance.

Reality: In a well-organized inclusive education program, paraprofessionals and special education teachers provide support to general education teachers. This support may be in the form of consultation, adaptations, modifications, team teaching, and paraprofessionals providing assistance under the direction of the supervising teacher in the classroom setting.

Myth: Inclusive education is not beneficial for general education students.

Reality: As school populations become more diverse, curriculum and materials are adapted, modified, or changed for students with special needs. These adaptations may be used to accommodate students who experience difficulties, at-risk students, and Title I students. Students in the general education classroom setting often are exposed to sign language, Braille, communication boards, medical devices, and special equipment. They learn at an early age that all children have the same kinds of thoughts and feelings, regardless of their limitations. Most important, they learn that they are more alike than different. A strong sense of community develops within the classroom environment.

Each inclusive setting is unique to the school system for which it is developed. An inclusive setting does not just occur naturally. The groundwork is in place before any students enter the classroom. Many students experience success in the classroom environment with the support of paraprofessionals, and it would be very difficult for students to be included in the classroom without this additional support. And the added support (although intended for students with special needs) helps all students. With an extra adult in the classroom, there are additional opportunities to individualize the instruction and monitor student progress. Paraprofessionals are also positive role models for students.

A small percentage of students require an alternative placement. In inclusive settings, a continuum of services is available and ranges from full-time classroom placements to full-time placement in a segregated setting, with many options in between. Alternate placement is available for students who are unable to make academic gains after assistance and modifications to the curriculum or environment have been implemented in the general education setting. Therefore, paraprofessionals may work with students in many capacities either in the classroom environment or in an alternative setting.

BENEFITS OF INCLUSIVE EDUCATION

Think about the negative feelings generated in the Inclusion/Exclusion activity earlier in this chapter. For the majority of students with special needs, inclusive education helps increase their self-esteem. No longer are they removed from the classroom to attend a special class, with a special teacher, in a special room. They view the classroom setting as a safe place to participate and take the risks that are necessary to learn and succeed.

Inclusive education supports the current educational system. In the general education classroom, modifications and strategies directed toward students with disabilities are beneficial to the general education students because they help improve and individualize the existing curriculum for all students.

Inclusive education encourages effective collaboration. No longer are there two separate educational systems. Rather, there is one united system, which is beneficial for the following reasons:

- Communication and collaboration increase with the new educational team.
- No individual is expected to have all the expertise required to meet the educational needs of all students in the classroom.
- When team members with knowledge in many diverse areas collaborate to problem solve, results are achieved more quickly.
- Inclusive education improves the quality of on-site training. Instead of providing separate inservice training for specific disabilities or modification strategies, the educational team learns together. Inservice training directly relates to individual students and is relevant because all members of the team have accepted ownership for the students. Team members learn by doing.
- Inclusive education benefits the majority of students. When two (or more) adults work collaboratively in the classroom, questions are answered quickly, projects are easily monitored, and all students receive more individualized attention. Students accept one another as contributing members of the school community.

Inclusive education is and will continue to be a controversial issue in education. Much time and energy continues to be dedicated to the debate over whether inclusive education is best for students. In the meantime, students with special needs are in the classrooms, and they need support. These students have a desire to learn, to be accepted, and to be successful. It is the job of the educational team to provide the appropriate service to students with the resources currently available.

NOTES

2

The Special Education System

*The great thing in this world is not so much where we stand,
but what direction we are moving.*

Oliver Wendell Holmes

Welcome to the world of special education! As a paraprofessional, you are a vital member of the special education team. This chapter provides an overview of the special education system, handicapping conditions, and some of the common characteristics of each disability.

STUDENT PLACEMENT

Student placement in the special education system occurs at various ages. Children with Down syndrome, orthopedic impairments, physical handicaps, and multiple disabilities are diagnosed early and begin to receive services within the first year of life. Children with hearing impairments, vision impairments, or autism frequently are diagnosed at a very young age by the parent or pediatrician or during a preschool screening. These children frequently receive services in an early intervention program.

The majority of students with learning disabilities, language disorders, mild mental retardation, and behavior disorders frequently begin receiving services in early elementary school. These disabilities become apparent as the demands of the curriculum increase.

Students are not simply placed into a special education program. To receive the additional services, they must meet specific guidelines and qualify for the services.

Parents are actively involved in each step of the process and may stop the process at any time. Although paraprofessionals are not involved in the formal process of assessment or writing individualized education plans (IEPs), a simplified narrative of the process follows.

The process usually begins with a referral to a team or group of professionals in the school. Typically, the classroom teacher makes the initial request due to concerns related to a student's performance in the classroom.

Once a referral is initiated, a multidisciplinary team meets to discuss the specific student and decide whether to proceed with an educational assessment. (A multidisciplinary team is a group of professionals and usually includes an administrator, a psychologist, a social worker, and teachers with various areas of expertise.) If the team determines that an assessment is needed, an assessment plan is developed. The formal assessment plan may include cognitive, social-emotional, academic, speech, and language assessments along with any additional areas that the team feels appropriate. The parents receive written notification that the school would like to begin to formally assess their child, and the parents must sign a consent form before the assessment can begin.

Once the parents give approval, various educational professionals begin to assess the student. This may include informal assessments, standardized tests, and classroom observations. When all of the assessments are complete, the team members (and parents) reconvene to compile the data and determine whether the student qualifies for special education services. If the student meets the federal guidelines, he or she qualifies for and can begin receiving special education services.

Together, the special education staff and the parents develop an IEP for the student, which is a legal document that summarizes all of the assessment findings and records specific student needs. Individual goals and objectives are developed, and the criterion is established for classroom support. Classroom accommodations and modification strategies are defined. The student's IEP is based on the student's needs, not the handicapping condition, and determines the type and amount of support the student will receive from teachers and paraprofessionals in the classroom setting.

Once the IEP is developed and signed, the school is obligated by law to provide the services that it details. The IEP is reviewed biannually and rewritten annually. A complete reassessment must occur every three years. This provision is a safeguard to ensure that progress is occurring and that students do not remain in the system if they no longer qualify for services.

WHAT ARE HANDICAPPING CONDITIONS?

Paraprofessionals new to the field often have questions related to a student's handicapping condition. Additional phrases that are used interchangeably with *handicapping condition* include *area of exceptionality* or *identified disability*. Some of the most frequently asked questions by those new to the field often include "What is the identified handicapping condition?" "What is the difference between the handicapping conditions?" and "How should students be served in relation to this disability?"

Special education is not a science, but guidelines do exist for placement and the guidelines must be adhered to. Characteristics between the various handicapping conditions often overlap, and there is no typical student with a learning disability, behavior disorder, language impairment, or other handicapping condition.

It is important to note that a handicapping condition or label does not determine the student's services, nor does it really tell much about the student. For example, not all students with learning disabilities have the same goals or receive the same amount of services. Each student is unique. Many identified students need accommodations to help compensate for their various exceptionalities. Often when people refer to those with disabilities, the focus is placed on the disability even though the disability is only a small part of the student as a whole.

Let us look at a very simple example. If you have prescription glasses, you have vision that is correctable with the glasses. The prescription glasses are used to correct your vision and allow you to see better. Because your vision is easily correctable with glasses, you would not qualify for special education services. However, if prescription glasses had not been invented, or you happen to have low vision that is not correctable with glasses, you would need specific accommodations in order to function. The current accommodation (glasses) is what separates you from a student with such vision. If prescription glasses were not available (or you forgot to bring them to class), you would require preferential seating to see the board, enlarged fonts or large-print books so that you would be able to do the required reading, and perhaps magnifiers to help with small-font material. Perhaps you would receive information auditorily by listening to the audio versions of your textbooks. Obviously, this does not mean that you cannot read, but that your eyes tire easily and therefore it is difficult to read for long periods. These simple accommodations allow you to learn the same as the others in the class and to function at the same level as those without glasses. Your vision has an effect on the way that some material is presented to you, but this disability does not define you as a person.

For many students, there is a fine line between whether or not they qualify for special education services. For some of those who do not qualify, simple accommodations enable them to function in the classroom. But some students qualify for services and may need more extensive accommodations and modifications. Therefore, it is important to remember that a disability is only a small part of the person, and many students with appropriate accommodations do very well in school.

When referring to students with special needs, *person first* language should be used. If you need to refer to a student with a disability, the correct terminology is to say, for example, "Mary has a hearing impairment" instead of "Mary is deaf" or "Rob has low vision" instead of "Rob is blind." This emphasizes that they are a person first (hence the concept's name) and the disability is a part but not all of them.

There are currently 13 areas of exceptionality in the federal law. It cannot be emphasized strongly enough that labels are only an identification tool. Once a student receives services, the label is secondary and rarely used. In fact, for many students you may not be aware of the handicapping condition unless you ask about it or have access to the student's IEP.

The terminology often varies between states; therefore, the following chart lists the terminology used in the federal law, and the text that follows discusses some of the more common terminology that is often used. If you would like additional information regarding definitions and criteria, I encourage you to contact the special education department at your school. In addition, the National Dissemination Center for Children with Disabilities has created informative and helpful fact sheets for each of the 13 disability categories. These fact sheets are available at www.nichcy.org.

Federal Terminology	
Autism	Additional areas served in this category include Pervasive Developmental Disorder (PDD), Rett Syndrome, and Childhood Disintegrative Disorder.
Deaf-Blindness	Combined hearing and visual impairment
Deafness	Deaf, hearing impaired, severe hearing impairment (Hearing loss may be slight, mild, moderate, severe, or profound.)
Emotional Disturbance	emotionally disturbed (ED) behavior disorders (BD) conduct disorder (CD) socially maladjusted
Hearing Impairment	hearing impaired (HI) hard of hearing
Mental Retardation	mentally retarded (MR) cognitive delay (CD) developmental delay (DD) mental handicap (MH) mildly impaired (MI) severely impaired (SI)
Multiple Disabilities	Includes a combination of impairments such as mental retardation and blindness, and mental retardation and physical disabilities.
Orthopedic Impairment	Includes congenital anomalies such as absence of a body part, impairments caused by disease such as tuberculosis or cerebral palsy, and amputations.
Other Health Impairments	Includes chronic or acute health problems such as asthma, attention deficit disorder, diabetes, and heart conditions.
Specific Learning Disability	learning disability (LD) learning differences (LD)
Speech and Language Impairment	speech and language impaired (SLI) Also includes communication disorders such as stuttering articulation, voice impairment, and language impairment.
Traumatic Brain Injury	traumatic brain injury (TBI)
Visual Impairment (including blindness)	low vision blind partially sighted

CLASSROOM IMPLICATIONS

Following is a brief description of each of the 13 handicapping conditions recognized under federal law. Although these are not applicable to all students, I have included some general classroom implications also.

Autism

Autism/Pervasive Developmental Disorder (PDD) is a developmental disability that occurs during infancy or early childhood. It is a behaviorally defined syndrome characterized by an uneven developmental profile, and it ranges from mild to severe. Children with autism vary widely in abilities, intelligence, and behavior, but many students with a mild form of autism do very well in the school setting. This disability significantly affects verbal and nonverbal communication and social interaction. Some of the characteristics of autism include irregularities and impairments in communication, engagement in repetitive activities and movements, resistance to change, and unusual responses to sensory experiences. Asperger's syndrome, Rett syndrome, and Childhood Disintegrative Disorder are diagnostic terms that are also related to autism.

Classroom implications: In general, these students require a well-structured environment with a predictable routine. It is important that they know in advance any changes in the daily routine or school day. In general, these students will learn better when information is presented visually as well as verbally. They may have difficulty interpreting facial expression, body language, and voice tone. It is important to create opportunities for these students to have structured social and collaborative interactions with the other students in the classroom and to provide many opportunities to practice socialization skills.

Deaf-Blindness

Deaf-blindness is defined as a simultaneous hearing and vision impairment. This combination often leads to severe communication and other developmental and educational problems. Due to the complexity of the disability, these students cannot be served solely under either the category of hearing impairment or that of vision impairment.

Classroom implications: These students need many specialized services coordinated by several specialists. These supervising teachers provide materials to you, the paraprofessional, to help these students. See also the following discussion of deafness and vision impairment, including blindness.

Deafness

Deafness is defined as a hearing impairment so severe that a child is impaired in processing linguistic information through hearing, with or without amplification, which adversely affects the child's educational performance. Hearing loss can be slight, mild, moderate, severe, or profound. Students identified as having a hearing impairment lack the ability to hear sounds and discern clarity, and their impairment may range from a slight hearing loss to deafness.

Classroom implications: Hearing loss or deafness does not affect these students' intellectual capacity or ability to learn, although they do require specialized services from various specialists based on their needs. The students may have an interpreter in the classroom because they need additional assistance with all information presented orally, including class lectures, note taking, and verbal direction.

Emotional Disturbance

Emotional disturbance is defined as a condition exhibiting one or more of the following characteristics over an extended period of time and to a marked degree that adversely affects a child's educational performance: an inability to learn that cannot be explained by intellectual, sensory, or health factors; an inability to build or maintain satisfactory interpersonal relationships with peers and teachers; inappropriate types of behavior or feelings under normal circumstances; a general pervasive mood of unhappiness or depression; and a tendency to develop physical symptoms or fears associated with personal or school problems. Characteristics may also include hyperactivity, aggression (toward self and others), withdrawal, immaturity, and learning difficulties.

Classroom implications: The education program for these students includes emotional, behavioral, and academic support. They may have intervention plans and behavior plans that need to be consistently monitored. Consistency in programming, definite limits, and expectations must be clearly defined for the majority of these students.

Hearing Impairment

A hearing impairment, which could be permanent or fluctuating, adversely affects a child's educational performance. A child with a hearing impairment generally can respond to auditory stimuli.

Classroom implications: Hearing loss does not affect intellectual capacity or ability to learn, although students with this disability generally require some form of special education services to receive an adequate education. They may receive speech and language services because they need support with oral directions, note taking, and the majority of information that is presented auditorily.

Mental Retardation

The degree of impairment for mental retardation can be mild, moderate, or severe. Students with mild to moderate impairment have below-average cognitive ability and therefore learn at a slower rate than their peer group. Functional skills also lag behind those of their peers. Students who are mildly mentally retarded will learn to read, write, and perform basic math, although it takes them longer to acquire these skills. A large discrepancy exists not only in the acquisition of academic tasks, but also in the students' growth both socially and emotionally.

Classroom implications: Students with mental retardation may have trouble paying attention, generalizing skills, applying previously learned skills to new situations, remembering information, using language, or thinking abstractly. Due to difficulty in learning, some students have low self-esteem or poor self-concept. They usually require large amounts of repetition to learn skills presented in the classroom.

Some students' cognitive abilities may fall in the area of severe or profound. These students experience extreme difficulty with academic learning and may have unique physical needs. Some students will exhibit behaviors such as tantrums, outbursts, and aggressive or passive behavior. Educational programs assist them with learning appropriate social behavior, self-help skills (including personal care or grooming), communication, functional academic skills, and independent living skills.

Multiple Disabilities

Multiple disabilities are defined as simultaneous impairments (e.g., mental retardation and blindness, mental retardation and orthopedic impairment), the combination of which causes such severe educational needs that they cannot be accommodated in a special education program solely for one of the impairments.

Classroom implications: Students with multiple disabilities have an educational program that incorporates a variety of components to meet their considerable needs. Various specialists and medical staff may be involved in meeting these needs. Students may require special equipment, communications devices, and assistive technology.

Orthopedic Impairment

Orthopedic impairments include those caused by congenital anomaly (e.g., clubfoot, absence of a body part), disease (e.g., poliomyelitis, bone tuberculosis), and other conditions (e.g., cerebral palsy, amputations, fractures or burns that cause contractures).

Classroom implications: Students with orthopedic impairments have a wide range of disabilities. Some students may need medical supervision, and others may need assistive technology and communication devices.

Other Health Impairments

Students identified in this area have limited strength, vitality, or alertness (due to chronic or acute health problems such as a heart condition, asthma, epilepsy, leukemia, diabetes, epilepsy, spina bifida, cerebral palsy, or amputations), which adversely affects their development or performance. This category is very broad, and some students with attention deficit disorder can receive services under this category. Along with physical and medical needs, some students have a secondary handicap such as a learning disability, a communication disorder, or a severe impairment.

Classroom implications: Due to the uniqueness of each handicap, these must be defined individually. Cognitive abilities range from below average to superior. Some students may have multiple handicaps or be confined to a wheelchair. Others require no special education services, with the exception of nursing services. Some students are frequently absent due to extensive medical care. The services provided by the special education department vary depending on each student's IEP. The special education department will provide information to you regarding these low-incidence handicaps.

Specific Learning Disability

The largest groups of students identified receive services under this category. Specific learning disability is defined as a disorder in one or more of the basic psychological processes involved in understanding or using language, spoken or written, that may manifest in an imperfect ability to listen, think, speak, read, write, spell, or do mathematical calculations. Conditions related to this category include perceptual disabilities, brain injury, minimal brain dysfunction, dyslexia, and developmental aphasia. Learning disabilities do not include learning problems that are the result of visual, hearing, or motor difficulties or of environmental, cultural, or economic disadvantage.

Classroom implications: For these students, difficulties may be apparent in the areas of reading, language arts, math, or language. Difficulties may occur in isolated areas or be evident across several areas of the curriculum. Expressive (speaking) or receptive (understanding) language can affect reading or the general acquisition of information. Visual discrimination of shapes, letters, and symbols also can be demanding, which makes copying from the board, reading, or writing difficult. Difficulties with auditory processing are also common, including the ability to follow multistep directions, discriminate between sounds, or express oneself verbally. Students may have trouble with fine motor skills (e.g., writing, cutting, pasting, drawing, holding a pencil) and gross motor skills (e.g., walking, running, catching or kicking a ball, skipping). Another area that may affect students' ability to learn is behavior. Some students are hyperactive, unable to focus, unable to stay on task, or unable to follow classroom routines. Social skills may also be inadequate.

A severe discrepancy between the students' cognitive (intellectual) abilities and their academic performance must be documented. Therefore, the majority of students with a learning disability have average to above-average cognitive ability, but fail to perform at an academic level that is commensurate with their perceived ability.

The profile of a student with a learning disability will show definite strengths and limitations in various academic areas. The student may excel in math yet struggle with reading and written language. The student may read fluently yet not comprehend the material due to difficulty in the acquisition of language. The student may have strong verbal skills and dominate classroom discussions yet be unable to write a simple sentence.

Speech and Language Impairment

Speech and language impairment is defined as a communication disorder such as stuttering, impaired articulation, a language impairment, or a voice impairment that adversely affects a child's educational performance. Language impairment can be in the area of expressive (speaking) or receptive (understanding) language, or students may experience a language delay.

Classroom implications: Many students identified in special education receive services for speech and language. Students who have trouble with receptive language often have difficulty understanding directions or oral presentations. Grammar, sentence structure, and vocabulary support are often required. Deficits in the area of expressive language may include articulation (substituting, omitting, distorting, or adding sounds) and fluency (stuttering) disorders. Some students are unable to organize their thoughts and ideas; their spoken language may be rapid and disorganized. Students with expressive language difficulty often feel uncomfortable participating in classroom discussions.

Traumatic Brain Injury

Traumatic brain injury is defined as an acquired injury to the brain caused by an external physical force, resulting in a total or partial functional disability of psychosocial impairment that adversely affects educational performance. The term applies to open or closed head injuries resulting in impairments in one or more areas such as cognition, language, memory, attention, reasoning, abstract thinking, judgment, information processing, and speech. The term does not include brain injuries that are congenital or degenerative or brain injuries caused by birth trauma.

Classroom implications: These students may need extra time to complete assignments and tests. They may need to relearn things previously known and may have difficulty grasping new concepts. They may also require medical care during the school day.

Visual Impairment (Including Blindness)

Visual impairment, including blindness, is defined as impairment that, even with correction, adversely affects a child's educational performance. The term includes both partial sight and blindness.

Classroom implications: Students with low vision may be able to see materials and objects that are close, but unable to see the blackboard, overhead, or distant objects. These students may need special devices such as lighting or magnifiers. Often mobility is a concern. Large and small motor development may also be delayed depending on the degree of impairment. These students may need support finding their way around the school, playground, or crowded areas.

Attention Deficit Disorder and Attention Deficit Hyperactivity Disorder

Two areas that receive a great deal of attention are attention deficit disorder (ADD) and attention deficit hyperactivity disorder (ADHD). Boys are more frequently diagnosed as having ADD/ADHD, and girls are commonly undiagnosed. Frequently, girls with ADD are overlooked and often thought of as daydreamers. Students diagnosed with ADD/ADHD are served in special education under the "other health impaired" label if the disability interferes with their ability to learn. More often than not, unless they have additional disabilities such as a specific learning disability, these children do not receive special education services but receive services through general education by the implementation of a 504 Plan, which the general education teacher and the parents develop together. A 504 Plan includes goals and objectives but differs from an IEP because a 504 Plan is meant to simply level the playing field by removing barriers as opposed to providing specific educational services. More often than not, you will have the opportunity to work with these students.

Some common characteristics of students with ADD include difficulty paying attention and remaining focused over a long period, consistent carelessness in daily assignments, inattentiveness during class, repeated misplacing of materials and supplies, and the inability to organize. Many of these students are easily distracted and forgetful in classroom settings. Students with ADHD may also fidget or talk excessively, have trouble remaining seated, incessantly blurt out answers, and frequently disrupt others. It is important to note that many of these characteristics apply to numerous students in the classroom and that not all students who exhibit these characteristics have ADD or ADHD.

Gifted and Talented Students

Students who are gifted and talented receive special education services if they have a secondary handicap that is part of the federal mandate. These students are often overlooked for special education services because they are frequently able to compensate for the disability during their educational careers. Students who are gifted and talented will not qualify for services if they are able to achieve at or above grade level. Periodically, you may work cooperatively with your school's gifted and talented educator if a student has a secondary diagnosis of a specific learning disability or a behavior disorder.

CONCLUSION

To qualify to receive services under the umbrella of special education, students must be assessed and meet specific criteria. The identification process is lengthy and comprehensive, and many students are referred to the special education team for assessment each year. Of the students assessed, many do not meet the predetermined qualifications and thus do not qualify for special education services. Those who meet the criteria are placed into special education. For many students it is a very fine line between qualifying for services and being expected to achieve without receiving them. Therefore, it is important to remember that all students are more alike than different. A label or handicapping condition does not define a student; it is only a means to receive additional support in the school setting.

NOTES

3

The Special Education Team

Never doubt that a small group of thoughtful, committed people can change the world; indeed, it's the only thing that ever has.

Margaret Mead

As a newly hired paraprofessional, this may be the first time you have entered a public school since your own graduation. For others, perhaps you volunteered in your child's classroom, chaperoned field trips, or helped teachers with various projects throughout the school year. Some of you may even have children with special needs and have extensive knowledge of the special education system.

The special education system is continually changing. The special education department is very different from the classroom environment because the entire department functions as one very large team. All major decisions are team decisions. A team develops a student's program, and the services are provided as a team. You are a part of this team, and your main responsibility as a paraprofessional is to help students by providing support under the direction of this team.

The students who receive support under the special education system receive services from a team of professionals, often referred to as the multidisciplinary team. The team consists of many members, and the members of each student's team change depending on the unique needs of the student. Special education teachers have various licensures. Some are licensed to teach students with mental retardation, others to teach students with specific learning disabilities, and some have multiple licensures. With a multidisciplinary team approach, all teachers are able to provide support to all students with special needs as long as at least one person on the team has the appropriate licensure related to the student's handicapping condition. For example, not all schools have a full-time teacher of the visually impaired because it is a low-incidence handicap. Therefore, this professional spends time traveling between schools. Because this specialist is not on location all the time, obviously he or she is unable to provide instruction to a particular student on a daily basis. Therefore, this specialist would attend the meetings for the student, provide materials, and consult with the classroom teacher, but a special education teacher on location administers the actual day-to-day services.

At a minimum, the members of a student's multidisciplinary team consist of the psychologist, the special education teacher, the classroom teacher, a parent or guardian, and an administrator. Listed here, in alphabetical order, are the staff members who may be part of the multidisciplinary team:

administrator

English as a second language teacher

general education teacher

hearing impaired teacher

nurse or health assistant

paraprofessional

parent or guardian

physical and occupational therapists

psychologist

social worker

speech and language clinician

special education teacher

vision teacher

vocational educator

The remainder of this chapter will help increase your understanding of the various multidisciplinary team members. The first paragraph describes the member's role on the team. The second includes comments related to the relationship that may occur between the paraprofessional and the team member. There is space at the end of each description for you to add more information and comments specific to your individual situation.

Administrator

The school administrator is a member of every educational team. The administrator makes administrative decisions, provides assistance with class schedules, coordinates inservice training for staff, and provides support in the development of inclusive settings. The administrator creates the positive environment necessary for inclusive schools.

The administrator oversees the entire special education department. Due to the size of this department, most administrators have one contact person, who is often referred to as the *lead teacher*. If you have questions, you should direct them to the lead teacher, who will convey the information to the administrator if needed. If the problem cannot be resolved, follow the proper channels in the department before setting up an appointment with the administrator. Some administrators have an open-door policy and welcome comments and concerns to be expressed directly.

_____

_____

_____

_____

English as a Second Language Teacher

The English as a second language (ESL) teacher assists students whose primary language is other than English. The ESL teacher's main role on the multidisciplinary team is to assist with the assessment of students who do not speak English.

If an ESL student is placed in special education, the ESL teacher will consult with you and provide appropriate modifications in conjunction with the special and general education teachers.

_____

_____

_____

_____

General Education Teacher

The general education teacher usually initiates the special education referral to the special education department either alone or in conjunction with a parent. The teacher has a wealth of valuable information regarding the academic progress and the social-emotional well-being of the student. The general education teacher also contributes information regarding the student's organizational skills, work habits, processing of information, and language. Once this information is compiled, a team decision is made regarding whether to proceed with the assessment. The classroom teacher's information also helps determine which specific areas should be assessed.

In an inclusive setting, a close relationship develops between the paraprofessional and the general education teacher. More often than not, you will work in the classroom under the guidance of the general education teacher, who will set the rules, guidelines, and expectations for the classroom. The expectations will be different for each classroom in which you work. The general or special education teacher will provide the instruction for the students, and your role in the classroom will vary depending on the documentation in the individualized education plan (IEP). It may include behavior management, reteaching or reinforcing skills, working with students in small groups, reinforcing self-help skills, assisting with mobility, and carrying out the modifications provided by the general and special education teachers.

_____

_____

_____

_____

Hearing Impaired Teacher

This teacher is responsible for the assessment of students with hearing impairments, which may range from mild to severe. The role of this specialist is to check hearing aids and adaptive devices and to provide direct instruction or consultation to the classroom teacher. Some students may require the services of a sign language interpreter.

The hearing specialist provides inservice, direct instruction, and help with strategies and ideas to accommodate students with hearing impairments within the classroom environment. If you work directly with these students, you may be required to learn how to use various adaptive devices in the classroom and provide academic support to the students.

_____

_____

_____

_____

Nurse or Health Assistant

The school nurse or health assistant screens students for vision and hearing; offers explanations of medical records and conditions; monitors prescription medicines; teaches specific health care skills; checks the fit, maintenance, and function of prosthetic and adaptive devices; and assists parents with medical referrals.

You may be involved with the school nurse or health assistant daily if a student takes medication, requires daily medical attention, or uses prosthetic and adaptive devices. If a student has an emergency medical plan, the nurse will be able to clarify the procedures for you.

_____

_____

_____

_____

Parent or Guardian

The parent or guardian is involved in each step of the educational process. To place a student in special education, a parent or guardian's signature must be obtained. He or she provides invaluable information relative to the child's strengths and limitations. Information relating to health, social or emotional levels, and other pertinent data contributes to the development of an appropriate educational program.

The supervising teacher will define your role in relation to the parent. You may be responsible for keeping a daily notebook to share with the parent. This notebook might include a daily activity update, a log of homework assignments, general comments regarding the day, or comments about the student's behavior. The special education teacher will tell you what and how to report. Your supervising teacher may also ask you to communicate with the parent by telephone on a regular basis.

_____

_____

_____

_____

Physical and Occupational Therapists

The physical therapist focuses on the assessment, training, and use of the lower extremities and large muscles. The occupational therapist focuses on the upper extremities and fine motor abilities.

Both therapists provide modification and the adaptation of materials. If special equipment is provided, you will be trained in how to use it correctly. Recommendations regarding the general classroom environment and suggestions for student accommodations will also be provided to you. As a paraprofessional, you may spend large amounts of time with students requiring the services of these therapists, and your observations are important to these specialists.

_____

_____

_____

_____

Psychologist

The school psychologist's expertise is in the administration and interpretation of standardized tests. The cognitive ability tests (intellectual functioning tests) are administered and scored by the psychologist. In addition, the psychologist may complete observations of students and their family history as well as compilation of student data. The psychologist is able to assist with the design and implementation of interventions and behavior management systems. He or she also acts as a resource for the building staff.

The psychologist may contact you for your observations regarding individual students. Feel free to contact the psychologist for information about child development, learning styles, or recommended reading materials on specific disabilities.

_____

_____

_____

_____

Social Worker

The social worker acts as a liaison between the home, the school, and community agencies. The social worker may counsel students and families, assess the effects of a student's home life on school performance, and assist families in emergencies. This specialist often is able to contribute valuable information regarding a student's social and emotional well-being that may affect the student's ability to learn.

The social worker may contact you for observations regarding specific students. If a student shares information with you about his or her safety, well-being, or family situation that may be harmful to the student, you should report it immediately to the social worker, supervising teacher, or administrator.

_____

_____

_____

_____

Speech and Language Clinician

The speech and language clinician determines whether language affects the learning in the classroom environment. The clinician's main role on the multidisciplinary team is to assess students for speech and language disorders. Once a student is in the program, the clinician works with the student to remediate articulation, voice, and fluency disorders or language (both expressive and receptive) difficulties.

The speech and language clinician assists with fostering communication skills in the general classroom environment. This specialist often provides supplemental materials and specific exercises to be implemented within the general education setting, and you may be responsible for implementing them. The clinician also provides ideas and materials for the reinforcement of language skills.

_____

_____

_____

_____

Special Education Teacher

The special education teacher is responsible for academic testing and student observations. When a student qualifies for placement, the special education teacher oversees the implementation of the student's program. Each special education teacher (case manager) is responsible for a specific group of students. The manner in which students are divided into groups depends on the individual school department. Some districts divide students by handicapping condition. In this case, teachers with a degree in learning disabilities only serve students who have been diagnosed with a learning disability. Teachers with a degree in serving the mildly impaired teach only students labeled as such. Other districts use a multidisciplinary team approach, allowing all special education teachers to work directly with all students as long as one member of the team holds the appropriate licensure and acts as a consultant.

The special education teacher is the first person with whom you will have contact. You may work with one or several special education teachers throughout the school day. Their role is to define your job and provide basic guidelines and expectations for individual students. They develop the appropriate adaptations and modifications, which you may be responsible for implementing. The special education teacher is responsible for seeing that the student's IEP is adhered to. Questions regarding the student's program should be directed to the special education teacher responsible for that specific student. If this teacher is unable to answer your questions, you will be referred to another member of the team.

_____

_____

_____

_____

_____

_____

_____

_____

Vision Teacher

The vision teacher assesses and provides modifications and adaptations for students with vision impairments, which may range from low vision to legal blindness.

The vision teacher often supplies enlargements, audiocassettes, large-print books, materials in Braille, assistive technology, and inservice as needed. If you have a student with a vision impairment in the general classroom, you will work closely with the vision teacher or consultant.

_____

_____

_____

_____

Vocational Educator

The vocational educator provides valuable information regarding students' work and career potential. The vocational educator offers job counseling, exposure to various jobs, assistance with job placement, and on-the-job coaching. The vocational educator works at the secondary level.

Under the direction of the vocational educator, you may assist students with the acquisition of skills necessary for job placement. You may also be responsible for monitoring, providing support, or overseeing a student on the actual job site.

_____

_____

_____

_____

Additional Staff Members

There may be additional staff members with whom you work. Use the following space to include any pertinent information that you would like to list.

_____

_____

_____

_____

_____

_____

_____

_____

Form 1, Contact List, a sample version of which is included here, offers a template to help manage the various team members with whom you have frequent contact. Make a copy of this form for your personal use. Include each team member's name, position, and contact information along with any additional notes.

Form 1: Sample Contact List

Name and Position	Contact Information	Notes
Mary Smith supervising special education teacher	msmith@xps.edu 612-000-1234	Contact with questions related to John, Joe, and Jane.
Randy Jones teacher of visually impaired	rjones@xps.edu 612-000-9876	Vision students. Comes once a week to see Sarah. Call on cell phone if needed because he works between various buildings.

The number of professionals involved with a given student's program depends on the disability and the amount of service required. For the majority of students, you will be involved with one supervising special education teacher and one general education teacher. If a student has severe or multiple disabilities, you will be in constant contact with many of the team members listed in this chapter.

NOTES

4

Confidentiality and Special Education

By constant self-discipline and self-control you can develop a greatness of character.

Grenville Kleiser

As a paraprofessional, you establish relationships with teachers, school personnel, students, parents, and the community. The quality of the relationships depends not only on your work performance, but also on the ethical behavior you demonstrate on the job. Ethics are particularly important because you are in a position of authority. You may encounter situations in which your interests, the student's interests, and the school's interests are in conflict. In these situations, consider the best interest of the individual student first.

An important aspect of ethical behavior is handling confidential information. Confidentiality is one of the most critical and important aspects of your job as a paraprofessional. It is your legal responsibility to observe the rights of both individual students and parents in regard to data privacy. The law protects the privacy of all students and their families.

During the course of a school day, you will receive information and perhaps overhear comments about family situations, behavioral issues, test scores, and a wide array of personal information. Although conversations related to students should take place in a private location, this does not always happen. Therefore, all information pertaining to a student (and family), whether shared directly with you or overhead, is confidential. Confidential information can only be shared if it is relevant to the student's education. Both state and federal laws regulate access to information related to students with disabilities, and the privacy of all student records is protected under the federal Family Educational Rights and Privacy Act (FERPA). Therefore, all documents pertaining to the student and the student's program are confidential. As a paraprofessional, you are required to uphold the ethics of confidentiality.

MANDATED REPORTING

As with all laws, there is always an exception, and sometimes a very important one. When working in the school, you will encounter certain situations that must be reported. For example, you are legally required to report suspected abuse or neglect. All states impose a civil or criminal penalty on those who do not report these incidents. The law requires any person who believes that a child is being or has been maltreated to report it to law enforcement or a child protection agency. All states have statues regarding the maltreatment of minors, and in most states your confidentiality is protected. For example, in Minnesota, Statue 626.556 states that paraprofessionals are required to report a suspected incidence of child abuse or neglect and that a person who reports child abuse or neglect in good faith is immune from any civil or criminal liability. If you encounter a situation of abuse or neglect, run—do not walk—to your supervising teacher, principal, or special education coordinator immediately. This is your responsibility, and you must report it.

CONFIDENTIALITY RELATED TO STUDENTS

The remainder of this chapter provides simplified answers to some very complex legal issues to increase your awareness of the legal issues that affect all adults working with children. This information is intended to serve as a guideline only and should not be construed as legal advice. School districts provide information on ethics and confidentiality during orientation, and if you have any questions in this area, it is best to meet with your supervising teacher.

Individualized Education Plan

The individualized education plan (IEP) includes information relevant to a student's performance in the areas of academics; communication skills; adaptive functioning skills; vocational assessment; and sensory, health, social, and emotional states. Psychological testing may also be included in this file. Each student has a yearly IEP. Therefore, the special education file includes the current and previous IEPs as well as review documents. These documents are part of the student's permanent file, which is often kept in a separate folder in the cumulative file. Some schools keep the file in a separate location to ensure the student's confidentiality. The procedural safeguards in the law require that when an IEP is reviewed, a log sheet must be signed and dated, and the reason for the previewing or removing the document must be documented. (The special education department will provide the proper procedure for your district.) Some special education departments encourage paraprofessionals to read the files for the students with whom they work, but the majority will share only the pertinent information that will help improve the working relationship between you and the student.

IEP Meetings

You may periodically attend an IEP meeting to share information regarding a student's performance in the classroom environment. During these meetings, parents frequently share personal and confidential information. Most personal information (e.g., a separation, a pending divorce, financial difficulties) is shared verbally, which helps the teacher understand the student. Usually, to avoid a temporary situation becoming part of the student's permanent file, this information is not documented. It is important to note that all information shared during an IEP meeting or any parent meeting is confidential.

The Special Education Department

The special education department is a department full of activity. Many school districts do not have the luxury of private conference rooms, so conversations and meetings often occur in the special education area. Often these meetings include social workers, psychologists, school nurses, and outside consultants. Any information that you may overhear during these meetings is also confidential.

The General Education Classroom

Previously, teaching was a solitary profession. The classroom consisted of one adult and a group of students, and teachers were accustomed to working alone for the greater part of the day. With inclusive classrooms, classroom dynamics have changed. The classroom teacher now has one, two, or more adults in the classroom at any given time, and not all teachers are comfortable in this situation. A good relationship is based on trust and mutual respect. It takes time to establish such a relationship, and the easiest way to damage it is to criticize, gossip, or discuss situations that occurred in the classroom with others outside of the classroom. Your role is to provide support to the special education students in the classroom.

As a paraprofessional, most likely you will work at a specific grade level or in a specific department. There may be times when you observe a specific teaching technique or the style of a lesson that will benefit others who are teaching the same subject matter. If this is the case, write it down and at an appropriate time ask the teacher if you can share the information. Most teachers will not mind. On the other hand, if the teacher receives a compliment or is questioned about the technique you shared (without his or her knowledge), the teacher may wonder what additional information you have shared and with whom.

In addition to doing so with the adults, you will develop a relationship with the students in the classroom. Establishing a trusting relationship is important. If you work with an individual student in the classroom, often the student will think of you as a confidant. If you have knowledge or even a suspicion that a student is physically, mentally, or sexually abused or neglected, you are required to report this information.

Paraprofessionals

Paraprofessionals are your colleagues. Most likely, you will have similar successes and experience the similar difficulties on the job. Perhaps you will work with some of the same teachers within the same classrooms. When sharing, respect the students and remember that confidentiality applies. With teachers, if there is an issue it should be discussed with the teacher and not with colleagues.

Parents

As a paraprofessional, you will have frequent contact with parents in both the school setting and the community. It is important to remember that confidentiality also applies outside of the school environment.

The best way to avoid any confrontation is to honor confidentiality for every student. For this reason, conversations regarding specific students must be confined to the school setting and occur only with adults directly involved with the student. If you are discussing your job outside of the school setting and happen to refer to a student, use only the first name. Better yet, simply refer to the student as "a student."

You should avoid sharing information about a student's progress with the parents or guardians unless the supervising teacher has provided you with specific directions. If parents ask questions about a student's IEP or other legal issues, ask them to contact the supervising teacher.

Special Education Students

Students in the classroom regularly have questions regarding their peers with special needs. At the elementary level, many books are available to explain the various disabilities in caring and compassionate ways. Look for disability awareness books by searching online or inquiring in the school's library or media center.

Children are curious by nature. Therefore, anticipate possible questions and discuss the topic with your supervising teacher. Often there is no need for elaborate responses. The supervisor can help determine the appropriate responses based on the age of the peers. The response to the question depends on the grade level. At the elementary level, some of the following questions will be asked:

"Why does Vanessa talk so funny? I can't understand her."

"Why does Kaman use a wheelchair, hearing aid, [etc.]?"

"Why do Bobby's eyes wiggle?"

"What's wrong with Mary?"

"How come you have to go to the bathroom with Natalie?"

"How come John gets all of the easy work?"

"Why does Susan make those funny noises?"

"How come you work with Joey and not me? I need help, too!"

Often, if a student has a severe disability, the school nurse, the special education teacher, or the parent will provide general information about the disability to the entire classroom. Disability awareness discussions are important because they allow students to ask questions and to understand. Many older students are comfortable with their disability and are able to explain and answer questions on their own.

Students often look to the adults for examples of how to interact. So it is important for adults to model patience, tolerance, and acceptance because students learn from these examples. When students ask direct questions, it is important to respect the rights and privacy of the student when answering. It is also important to emphasize to students that they are more alike than different.

ACTIVITIES

The following activities encourage you to think about situations related to confidentiality. These activities are often part of an orientation or a problem-solving session. If you are completing them individually, discuss your responses with your supervising teacher. Although hypothetical, these are common situations based on feedback from paraprofessionals. In each case, read the paragraph and answer the question. Possible responses to the question are found at the end of each activity. **Form 2, Discussion Activities for Paraprofessionals,** includes additional activities. If completing the activities in a group, be sure to add situations that you have encountered. Odds are that if you have experienced it, others will also.

Activity 1: The Teachers' Lounge

Ms. Allen is a paraprofessional who works in a second-grade classroom. She spends the majority of her day with Josh, a student with behavior problems who reacts strongly to change. Earlier this morning, Ms. Allen was told that Josh's parents have just separated. During lunch, Josh explodes. He throws his lunch tray at Ms. Allen and yells, "I hate you as much as I hate my parents!"

When the incident is over and Josh has calmed down, Ms. Allen joins a group of colleagues for lunch. Much to her surprise, Josh is the topic of their conversation. Ms. Allen does not comment and quietly eats her lunch. As she prepares to leave, one of her colleagues asks her what is going on and if it is true that Josh's parents have separated. If you were Ms. Allen, what would you do?

Possible response: When Ms. Allen realized her colleagues were discussing Josh, she should have explained immediately that it is a breach of confidentiality to discuss the student. No response is often construed as support. When asked by her colleagues about the parents' separation, an appropriate response would be that she is unable to discuss the student's family life.

Activity 2: In the Community

Mr. James is a paraprofessional at a middle school. In the afternoon, he works as a trainer in the weight room at the local athletic club. The father of one of his students works out in the weight room every afternoon, and they have become friends. He repeatedly asks Mr. James about his son's progress in school. If you were Mr. James, how would you respond?

Possible response: This can be a difficult situation because Mr. James works directly with the student and is an acquaintance of the father. One response is to provide general positive information, for example, he is working very hard, he is a great kid, and so on. If the father persists with questioning, Mr. James can ask him to set up an appointment with the classroom teacher and say that he would be very happy to attend also. He may also explain that he does not like to discuss any student outside of the school setting.

It is important to remember that you are a professional and that professionals honor confidentiality in all settings. It is not only out of respect for the student and family that emphasis is placed on confidentiality; it is also the law. As an employee of a school district, you always need to respect the privacy and confidentiality of your coworkers, your students, and your students' families.

GUIDELINES FOR CONFIDENTIALITY

- Discuss students only with people who have the right to that information. Avoid discussing students with anyone else.

- Do not offer information when you are unsure whether it should be considered confidential. When in doubt, it is best to say nothing. Simply state that you cannot answer that question, or refer the person to the special education teacher.
- Do not keep personal notes or files on individual students. If you must keep this information, it should be in a folder that is placed in a file cabinet or other secure location.
- Do not remove personal files without following the proper procedure.
- Do not discuss staff members, department issues, or student issues with any school-based personnel if they are not directly involved in the situation.
- If you are talking about your job in a social setting, do not use student names during the conversation.
- Use good judgment.
- Report all suspicions of neglect or abuse immediately.

The legal and ethical duties of a paraprofessional working in a school system are important. This entire chapter is easily summarized by a few key phrases: maintain confidentiality; show respect for colleagues, students, and their families; and demonstrate dependability and integrity for student differences!

NOTES

5

Getting Started

Choose a job you love and you will never have to work a day in your life.

Confucius

Paraprofessionals are an integral part of the special education team, and without them an inclusive education program is difficult to implement. Some of the benefits of involving paraprofessionals in providing services to students with special needs include the following:

- expanded learning opportunities for students with disabilities
- opportunities for more individualized instruction
- increased ability to monitor and evaluate students with disabilities
- greater consistency in services for students
- more opportunities for vocational skill development

Paraprofessionals provide support in many areas of inclusive education; therefore, the job responsibilities for one paraprofessional may be completely different from those of a colleague. A few paraprofessionals may provide support to one student for the entire school day, whereas others may work in a classroom with a variety of students, transition between classrooms, or work in a resource room setting. Some paraprofessionals have clerical responsibilities such as compiling data, record keeping, and general office duties. The special education department is unique, and jobs are constantly changing.

When working in an inclusive setting, it is important to maintain a positive attitude (especially during stressful times) with both students and colleagues. Your attitude is contagious to those around you. When you are positive, students and staff with whom you interact are more likely to be positive. The job is demanding, but the rewards are great!

LEARNING ABOUT POLICIES AND PROCEDURES

Orientation is a perfect time to have all of your questions answered. Your hire date often determines whether you will have a formal or informal orientation. Formal orientations occur in the fall when there are numerous new hires. For those hired midyear, an individual, informal orientation occurs, often provided by the special education department.

Building Orientation

Prior to working with students, an orientation to the building and members of the school community will take place. A tour of the school building highlighting frequently used places such as the media center, gymnasium, lunchroom, faculty/break room, and adult and student bathrooms is a time saver. Introductions to key people in the building will also occur. The following are a few items that may be addressed in this type of orientation:

Adult computers. What is the policy regarding school computers for staff members? What is the policy regarding personal e-mail and Internet use?

Cafeteria. What is the procedure for students purchasing hot lunch or bringing their lunch? Are the procedures different for students than they are for adults?

Media/technology center. What is the procedure for checking out material for student use? What is the procedure for checking out adult resources?

Office. Where do I retrieve/send mail? What are the policies regarding reproduction of materials? Where are student files located, and what is the procedure for accessing this information if needed?

Some policies and procedures are districtwide, and others pertain to individual buildings. If you do not receive an employee handbook, be sure to address the following:

- What is the school discipline plan, and how is it enforced? (A schoolwide policy is usually in place to ensure consistency within the common areas of the school.)
- What is the procedure if a building evacuation or building lockdown occurs? (Where are the exits, and what is the procedure in case of a fire, tornado, bomb threat, or any other situations that might occur?)
- How is a medical emergency handled? Is it handled the same if it occurs in the classroom, hallway, lunchroom, or playground? (What is the procedure if a child falls and breaks a bone, has a seizure or an asthma attack, and so on?)
- What is the procedure if a paraprofessional is sick and unable to come to work? (How are absences reported? Is there a callboard for substitute paraprofessionals?)

THE PARAPROFESSIONAL'S ROLE

The individualized education plan (IEP) determines the paraprofessional's role. This legal document spells out the amount of direct and indirect service that a student receives from the special education department.

The supervising teacher is responsible for direct instruction, and the paraprofessional is required to carry out instructions provided by the supervising teacher or the special education team. This may include working directly with students, reinforcing and reteaching of previously taught skills, data collection and documentation, and behavior management. The paraprofessional's job description may also include lifting, helping students with personal care, or assisting them with mobility. The following areas (listed in alphabetical order) include responsibilities carried out by paraprofessionals:

Behavior Management

- help students to stay on task
- collect data and document behaviors
- maintain daily logs or journals
- manage behavior charts
- follow up with rewards and consequences

Clerical Duties

- routine office duties (e.g., filing, typing, photocopying, answering the phone)
- maintain the database
- update teacher and student schedules

Data Collection

- collect and chart data obtained over specific time periods
- document student progress
- transfer and record classroom data

Develop Materials (under the direction of a supervising professional)

- create individualized learning materials
- modify existing curriculum materials
- record materials on audiocassettes

Health-Related Services

- assist with lifting and rotating
- assist with personal hygiene, including feeding and diapering
- assist with motor or mobility limitations
- use specific medical equipment

Organization Skills

- help students organize desks and lockers
- at the beginning of the day, help students unpack book bags and turn in homework
- at the end of the day, help students pack homework and the correct textbooks
- monitor specific students for organization skills

Reinforcement of Skills

- provide remedial instruction
- reteach previously taught skills
- play educational games

Supervision

- oversee small groups of students in the classroom
- monitor work completion
- supervise students during lunch, recess, and getting on and off the bus
- monitor students in common areas such as hallways

Team Participation

- communicate with parents regarding homework or daily activities
- communicate with general education and special education teachers
- attend student conferences and IEP meetings
- attend all required meetings

Work With Students (large- and small-group or individual)

- help students with activities
- help students with make-up work
- help students with interpreting and following directions
- administer individual tests
- monitor and assist students during seatwork activities
- support students with daily assignments (in all areas)
- read aloud to students or provide support for independent reading

No matter what your job description is, the supervising teacher is responsible for providing direction, guidance, and feedback related to your job duties and responsibilities. At times, you may have more than one supervising teacher. **Form 3, Job Description,** includes the previous list of possible duties in a checklist format. The purpose of this form is to help you keep track of your various job responsibilities, and it includes additional space to add responsibilities that may not be on the list. Fill out the form with your supervising teacher(s). If you have more than one supervising teacher, it is important that each teacher is aware of the expectations of the others. If you have too many responsibilities, ask to schedule a meeting with all of your supervising teachers to analyze the schedule and responsibilities together.

Your job description and duties will vary depending on the students served and the type of support needed to enhance the educational program. Once your job description is defined, **Form 4, General Responsibilities,** can be filled out to define individual responsibilities. In the following example of Form 4, a paraprofessional noted two areas in which training is needed, both of which include a follow-up date. If there are requirements that you feel that you are unable to perform, or if you are not sure how the teacher would want you to perform certain tasks, ask for clarification. In addition, if at any time you do not feel comfortable with the expectations, do not be afraid to speak with your supervising teacher. Be assertive and ask questions up front.

Form 4: Sample General Responsibilities

Paraprofessional Responsibility	Training Needed	Follow-Up Date
Reinforce skills taught by the general education teacher	no	
Administer individual tests	no	
Implement teacher-designed materials with individual or small groups of students	no	
Assist student with motor or mobility limitations	yes	10/01, or prior to working with student
Supervise student during lunch and recess	no	
Assist student with personal care	yes	10/01, or prior to working with student

ROLE DELINEATION

There is a clear delineation of roles between the classroom teacher and the paraprofessional. In the classroom environment, some responsibilities should not be assigned to paraprofessionals. For example, the paraprofessional should never be solely responsible for a classroom if the supervising teacher is absent, creating lesson plans, or providing the initial instruction to students. As a paraprofessional, you may reteach and provide reinforcement, but the classroom or special education teacher should provide the initial instruction. You can use **Form 5, Roles and Responsibilities,** to document the teacher activity, the paraprofessional activity, or both. Later, you can follow up with the supervising teacher for role clarification. The following is a comparison of roles in various situations:

Form 5: Sample Roles and Responsibilities

Supervising Teacher	Paraprofessional
Develops the weekly lesson plans	Reinforces the lessons under the guidance of the supervising teacher
Determines the objective for the lesson	Provides support to students to help meet the lesson objective
Provides instruction for the class, small groups, and individuals	Reinforces the lesson and provides drill and practice activities
Assigns silent reading activity to entire group of students	Reads materials aloud to individuals or a small class
Administers essay tests to all students	Writes the narrative that a student dictates
Develops with student and parents a specific plan for daily homework completion	Monitors the daily homework plan with the student

(Continued)

Form 5 (Continued)

Supervising Teacher	Paraprofessional
Implements medical schedules with nurse or nursing assistant	Accompanies the student (if necessary) to health room to accommodate medical needs
Plans and initiates conferences with parents	Participates in the conferences, if appropriate
Plans behavior management strategies for individual students and groups	Implements behavioral strategies using the same techniques as the teacher; monitors and documents information

DEVELOPING A SCHEDULE

When the job description is determined, it is time to create a daily schedule in collaboration with the general and special education teachers. You may rotate between classes, work in one classroom, or spend small amounts of time in several classrooms. Perhaps the schedule includes support in a computer class for one student, a physical education class with another, and lunch with a third. Each schedule is different due to the unique needs of the students. **Form 6, Daily Schedule,** is a template that can be used to create

Form 6: Sample Daily Schedule

Time	Location	Activity	Supervising Teacher
9:30–9:40	Classroom 1 Room 200	Pick up student from bus	P.C.
9:45–10:00	Classroom 2 Room 206	Homework completion Daily schedule overview	H.P.
10:05–11:00	Classroom 3 Room 108	Language Arts—Reteach— Read aloud with students	P.C.
11:00–12:00	Gym Room 131 Room 132	Mon.—Phys. Ed. Tues.—Art Class Wed.—Computer Class Monitor student behavior during class	L.S
12:00–12:30	Lunch		
12:30–1:10	Lunchroom	Lunchroom and playground duty	P.C.
1:10–1:30	Prep time Consultation		
1:30–2:00	Classroom 2 Room 206	Reading block	K.R.
2:00–3:00	Classroom 4 Room 110	Math class Drill and reinforcement Supplemental curriculum provided by special ed. teacher	P.C. and H.R.

your schedule. Form 6, Sample Daily Schedule, on page 40 is an actual schedule for a paraprofessional who works in multiple classrooms throughout the day.

A daily schedule is needed because time blocks and classrooms change. The previous example does not include student names. If you need to list specific students, use initials in case the schedule is misplaced. (Remember confidentiality!) Once the schedule is complete, try it for several days to determine the effectiveness (and problems) and make the necessary changes. Often a schedule looks workable on paper but once implemented the allocation for transition times ends up too short or it takes much longer to attend to a student's medical needs. The only way to know is to try it. It can take several weeks of adjustments to create a workable schedule. Finally, just when it is perfect, a new student is added to a program or a student requires a change in program and everything changes! Flexibility and patience are great virtues for paraprofessionals.

Once the schedule is set, it is important to follow it and at the time indicated. There may be times when you arrive at the designated time and classroom instruction is taking place. If this is your scheduled time, do not leave the classroom. Use the time to observe the students in the classroom setting. During these observation times, anticipate what support the students will need. Take notes; write key vocabulary words, main ideas, or lesson reinforcement questions to use as a follow-up with students. Perhaps the time can be used for paperwork such as observation reports, updates to communication logs, or curriculum modifications. This time is valuable for the general education teacher as well. The teacher is able to monitor and adjust the assignment, deviate from the lesson plan if needed, or terminate the lesson early without having to wait until later to provide you with an explanation.

SCHEDULING FOR A SUBSTITUTE

Once the master schedule is complete, it is time to prepare a substitute folder. Because job responsibilities vary and perhaps you work with many teachers, a substitute folder is essential. If your responsibilities include working with students who have specific medical or health needs, it is important to have a trained colleague who is able to take care of these needs in your absence. This should be discussed with the supervising teacher.

A substitute folder should include the daily schedule, a map of the school with emergency exits and the individual classrooms highlighted, and, most important, a contact person who can clarify questions about your daily responsibilities. Following are some additional items that may or may not be applicable to your position:

Bus duty. If your job entails supporting students with transportation issues, list the students along with the bus number and the approximate time of pick-up and delivery to the bus. Include any special instructions. Pictures of individual students are helpful for the substitute, especially if the substitute is required to meet the students upon arrival.

Special medical or personal concerns. You may be responsible for reminding students about medication, escorting students with special health needs such as feeding tubes or catheters to the health room, or taking care of personal issues such as diaper changing. Be sure to provide a list with these students' names, classrooms, and the time when such assistance occurs.

Classroom duties. In terms of academic assistance in the classroom, list the class, time, room number, and names of the general and special education teachers. List the first names of the students you are responsible for overseeing, and, if needed, write general comments regarding each student. Some students have trouble with transition and a change in routine.

Students with special concerns. If you anticipate an adverse reaction to a substitute from a specific student, discuss the situation with the general education teacher. This teacher often provides the program consistency needed while you are absent. Many times, there are changes in the daily classroom curriculum that you will not be aware of. The general education teacher will guide the substitute when you are absent.

Emergency medical or behavior plans. If there are emergency medical plans or alternative behavior plans for specific students, attach copies to your schedule.

Lunchroom. If you attend lunch with a specific student, provide the name of the student and the reason for attending lunch (e.g., student needs support in the lunch line, student has a tendency to choke, student needs help with outerwear).

Organize all of this information, create the substitute folder, and provide a copy to your supervising teacher. Some school districts require a copy for the main office also.

EFFECTIVE COMMUNICATION STRATEGIES

Paraprofessionals are a valuable asset to the classroom, and most teachers welcome the additional support. Working together in a team situation requires frequent and open communication. Engaging in effective communication is a critical and complex skill that is often taken for granted. The assumption is that everyone communicates effectively, but this is not always the case.

Verbal Communication

One component of effective communication is speaking. It is important to speak clearly so that others can easily understand what you are saying. When providing information to colleagues verbally, it is important to report specific observations and to be as objective as possible. Describe what you have seen or heard, but avoid drawing conclusions.

Teachers' use of technical language often isolates paraprofessionals from conversations. In special education, acronyms are frequently used, many of which you will not be familiar with. The special and general education teachers should make every attempt to explain the language and specific terminology used, but because they often use it unconsciously, do not be afraid to ask for clarification. You in turn should attempt to learn some of the common terminology and acronyms that are frequently used in education. If you encounter unfamiliar terminology that is consistently used during meetings (or during a time when you cannot receive clarification), write down the terms and ask later. **Form 7, Special Education Acronyms,** references the most common acronyms used in special education.

The second component of communication is listening. To be an active listener, you need to focus on what the person is saying. If a direction is not clear, paraphrase it; do not hesitate to ask questions when clarification is needed.

Keep your focus on what the speaker is saying. It is common for many adults to think about and make predictions about what is going to be said before the speaker has finished. Often when this happens, the receiver has started to anticipate his or her turn to speak and is mentally rehearsing a response, thereby missing part of what the speaker has actually said.

The following tips will help you communicate more effectively and develop a positive role in working with teachers:

- Think before you speak.
- Listen well enough to ask related questions about the topic.
- Put as much energy into listening to others as you do into speaking to others.
- Paraphrase what you understand others to be saying.
- Observe what times of the day are best for individual interactions.
- Ask how to do the task and not why you need to do it.
- Avoid using words such as *always* and *never.*
- Use "I" statements when speaking.
- Observe others who speak, and note the qualities you admire. Select some of these qualities, and try to incorporate them when you are speaking or listening.
- Most important, do not be afraid to ask for clarification if you do not understand something, and do not be offended when asked to clarify a point that you have made.

As a paraprofessional, it is imperative to develop effective communication skills because the job entails working with a variety of different teachers, colleagues, and parents.

Written Communication

Written communication is another important aspect of your job. You will be responsible to report to the special education teacher regarding student performance in the classroom. With your insight, the special and general education teachers will continue to review and revise overall plans for the student. There are several methods of reporting and providing information to your supervising teacher, and this feedback may occur daily, weekly, or monthly.

Daily Communication

Whether you are assigned to one or several classrooms, finding time to discuss concerns and clarify lessons or activities daily is essential for a well-run program. It is important to schedule a specific time to meet each morning and to honor this time. A daily five-minute conversation with the classroom teacher (before the students arrive) will help the day progress efficiently. At times, the supervising teacher will need to make changes to lesson plans or modify the daily schedule due to unforeseen circumstances. It is important that you be aware of these changes because they will affect your schedule. If you are unable to meet with the teacher, it may be a surprise if you show up for class and the classroom is empty!

If you spend your day working in the general education setting, you need to communicate frequently with the supervising special education teacher. Often you are the connection between the student and the special education teacher, and it is next to impossible to meet with every teacher, every day. Therefore, you may meet with the supervising teacher weekly and keep a written log daily to bridge the communication gap. **Form 8, Daily Log,** is one form of communication that can be used to document information on an individual student or a group of students throughout the day. The following sample includes documentation for several students. Keeping confidentiality in mind, a log for the entire school day can be used if you are working with only one supervising teacher.

Form 8: Sample Daily Log

DAILY LOG

Student: Dana   **Date**: Feb. 3 **M T W TH F**

9:30 Dana was able to remove outerwear with the assistance of a peer (third time this week). He prefers to have peer support instead of adult assistance.

Student: Sharon **Date**: Feb. 3 **M T W TH F**

10:00 Sharon is unable to keep up with the daily science assignments. She is struggling with the reading. She tends to anger easily and is frustrated. Should the assignments be read aloud? Modified in length? Or the requirements for the number of assignments be modified?

Student: John   **Date**: Feb. 3 **M T W TH F**

12:00 Ms. Johnson received a phone call from the transportation office regarding John on the bus. Please see her ASAP.

Student: Mary   **Date**: Feb. 3 **M T W TH F**

1:00 Mary has been asked to leave the art class twice this week for hitting, poking, and disrupting the class. Please see the art teacher before the next art class, which is Tuesday of next week.

Student: Susan   **Date**: Feb. 3 **M T W TH F**

2:00 Math class is running smoothly. Susan is participating more with the problem-solving activities. (Today she raised her hand 3xs). She has completed the alternate curriculum, and I will need more supplemental curriculum (or instruction of how to proceed) by Thursday, Feb 5.

Thanks, M.J.

With written communication, it is important to remain objective. Always include the student's name, the time, the day, and the setting. As a paraprofessional, you may work with the student for only a small portion of the day, whereas the special education teacher is responsible for the student's entire program. The notes on this simple log provide valuable insight and information, which helps the special education teacher piece together the student's program. From the simple comments on the form, the special education teacher may conclude the following information:

> During the 9:30 time block, it was noted that Dana was able to remove his coat (for the third time) with peer support. This is important because it indicates that Dana is becoming more independent and asking for assistance from a friend instead of depending on an adult. If a goal on Dana's IEP is to become more independent and take care of removing his outerwear without the help of the paraprofessional, he may be moving toward meeting this objective by asking a peer to help with the task he is unable to complete alone.
>
> At 10:00, it was noted that Sharon has been experiencing difficulty in science. This note may indicate that the curriculum is becoming too difficult or that perhaps the science vocabulary and the reading level are too high in this specific textbook.

Perhaps Sharon will need additional support in this class. Another question that may arise is whether she is having difficulty with reading in other academic areas or whether she is only having trouble with the science textbook.

At 12:00, the general education teacher received a telephone call from the transportation department regarding Jim. Due to privacy, there are no details listed on the form. If this were extremely urgent, an immediate telephone call to the special education teacher would have occurred instead of asking for a meeting. Therefore, this note indicates that the special education teacher will need to follow up.

At 1:00, Mary was asked to leave class for the second time this week. Because this seems unusual for her, several questions may arise. Is Mary only acting out during this class? Is she having trouble with her peers in the class, or is something happening at home that the school is unaware of?

At 2:00, it was noted that Susan needs additional supplemental materials that are provided by the special education teacher. In this case, the paraprofessional is asking for additional materials with several days of anticipation. The special education teacher can determine whether Susan's work is too easy, whether she is ready to move on to another level, or whether she is able to participate more in the general education curriculum.

Form 9, Daily Communication, can be used for short notes or isolated incidents, such as in the following example:

Form 9: Sample Daily Communication

Student's Name: M. Jones	**Date:** April 15

Daily notes or comments: Mary arrived to school at 10:00 am (3x this week).

☑ See me regarding this
☐ Speak to the classroom teacher
☐ Call the parent
☐ _____

Both Forms 8 and 9 may be used for all curriculum areas. In addition to reporting the areas of difficulty, it is also essential to list the areas where the student has experienced success. This will help the team adjust the curriculum.

For students with behavior difficulties, Forms 8 and 9 will help identify specific areas of concern. Often, difficult students tend to be disruptive at specific times or only during certain class periods. This valuable information is provided to the special education teacher so that modifications to the curriculum or environment can be made for the student.

Due to confidentiality, keep the form in a file folder or put it into an envelope for the special education teacher. Do not just lay it on the desk of the classroom teacher or special education teacher. If a meeting is scheduled, you can share your direct observations about the student. If there is an area of immediate concern, you will need to set up a meeting to explain the situation.

As the team develops, you will be able to cover more information during the allotted time. When meeting with the special education teacher, keep in mind that each special education teacher is often responsible for supervising several paraprofessionals in addition to working with students, so conversations should emphasize the most important areas. It is a good idea to make a list of items that you would like to discuss prior to any meetings.

Some students have specific medical or behavior concerns and need alternate behavior or medical plans. These students must have an alternate plan in place. Paraprofessionals working with these students should review these forms frequently, and if updating is needed, it is the responsibility of the appropriate supervising teacher. Often schools have special forms to communicate these needs, and when available, the official forms should always be used. So before creating your own, check with the supervising teacher.

It is imperative to anticipate a problem and be prepared, instead of discovering during an emergency that there is no plan is in place. **Form 10, Alternate Plan,** is a form that should be filled out by the supervising teacher. This type of form is frequently used for students who are unable to follow the classroom rules, students who are consistently disruptive in the classroom, and students with severe behavior problems. All adults who provide services to such students should have a copy of the plan. For the majority of students, the plans are rarely implemented, but if you do need to use it, it will be in place and you will be prepared.

Students who have specific medical needs often have special procedures that need to be followed, and the school usually has a form on file for these students. If not, **Form 11, Medical Alert Form,** should be filled out by the nurse at the beginning of the school year. As a paraprofessional responsible for a student's safety, you must have a clear understanding of the exact procedures to follow should an emergency arise. Form 11 may be reproduced and used for students with allergies or those prone to seizures, choking, or malfunction of various medical devices.

Forms 10 and 11 should be kept in a readily accessible file, and all professionals who are involved with the student should have copies. If a situation arises and a medical or behavior plan is implemented, the special education teacher must be contacted immediately. Do not wait until the end of the day.

Weekly Communication

You will consistently take notes and write observations pertaining to students over the course of the week. Some departments schedule a weekly meeting to discuss general concerns related to students. Weekly meetings are also scheduled to discuss upcoming units, lesson plans, accommodations, and modifications. As you become familiar with the students, you will notice that the modifications and adaptations tend to fall into similar patterns for each student, and you will become familiar with those that are used consistently with each student.

Monthly Communication

During monthly meetings, the agenda may include setting long- and short-term goals and developing curriculum modifications. Do not save daily observations or questionable issues regarding individual students for monthly meetings.

OBSERVATIONS AND EVALUATIONS

Observations and formal evaluations are additional forms of communication. Their purpose is to provide direction, guidance, and feedback on your job performance. It may be required that an administrator, a special education professional, or a peer mentor observes while you work with students. These observations provide positive comments related to your skills and your interaction with students. Some school districts require one or two observations per calendar year, and some require every employee to develop long-term goals. These goals may be written in conjunction with the supervising teacher or on your own. The following are examples of such goals:

- Increase communication with special and general education teachers.
- Attend a class in relation to a specific disability.
- Become proficient in the use of specific adaptive devices.
- Try one new technique with a specific student per week.
- Keep a list of successful modifications for a specific student.
- Attend a CPR course.

The special and general education teachers will offer additional suggestions that are appropriate for your position, including specific classes, inservices, and medical training offered by the district.

BREAKDOWN IN COMMUNICATION

There are times when a breakdown in communication occurs. Inevitably, when people work together, they have different or preconceived notions of the outcome. It is important that people have effective ways of dealing with different perspectives and personalities in potentially conflicting situations. If you encounter a difficulty with a coworker, first meet with the individual to discuss your concern. During this meeting, identify the problem. Use "I" messages to communicate your feelings. The person may not even be aware that a problem exists. Define the problem, and look for possible solutions. The majority of problems are easily solved.

You should always try to work out the problem to the best of your ability before involving others. If you cannot figure out how to resolve the problem, the next step is to contact your supervising teacher, who will advise you of the proper procedure to follow.

CONCLUSION

The first few days of a new job are always hectic—so much to learn! Orientation, a new environment, new faces, and, of course, smiling students. Without you, the paraprofessional, an inclusive program is difficult to implement. Your job description covers such a wide range of responsibilities. Communication is important, and it is often difficult because there is limited time for it during the day. Hopefully, some of the ideas presented here will help facilitate communication. As a paraprofessional, you are often the bridge between the general education class and the special education department. As you become familiar with the new environment, the students and their needs, and the teachers with whom you work, the job will become easier!

NOTES

6

The Paraprofessional and the General Education Teacher

People have one thing in common: they are all different.

Robert Zend

In the past, general education and special education students received their instruction in two separate classrooms with two separate curricula. But the implementation of inclusive programs has changed the classroom environment considerably. Teachers who were accustomed to working in isolation in their individual classrooms often no longer do so. Frequently, paraprofessionals, special education teachers, and consultants come in and out throughout the school day. Some classroom teachers feel uncomfortable teaching in front of their colleagues; some feel as though they are in a fishbowl, constantly under observation. The frequent interruption from people coming and going all day long sometimes distracts the teaching and learning process.

WORKING IN THE CLASSROOM ENVIRONMENT

Consistency is especially important for students receiving support from different adults during the school day. A student with special needs often requires more consistency, yet due to the number of specialists who work with the student, his or her program often lacks consistency. **Form 12, Classroom Information**, can help bridge the gap. It provides a place to list pertinent information such as daily schedules, rules, and general information. By completing this form with the classroom teacher, you will have an understanding of how the classroom operates.

Periodically, a student will be unable to follow the classroom rules. This student may have an alternate discipline plan that is developed as part of his or her individualized education plan (IEP) or as a separate document. In both circumstances, the alternate plan often replaces the classroom behavior plan. If an alternate plan is developed (see Form 10), all adults involved with the student must receive a copy.

Establishing a Work Area and Supplies

The classroom arrangement is conducive to the classroom teacher's teaching style. It is flexible so as to accommodate the wide variety of activities that occur daily in the classroom. There will be times when the teacher is providing large-group instruction and you are involved with a small group of students in a separate area. From time to time, you will create student material, correct papers, or document information for the special education teacher. Given this wide variety of duties, you will need a workspace in each classroom. Your personal space may consist of a teacher's desk, a small table, or perhaps a student desk. Some paraprofessionals use portable carts, which keep all materials within reach and can easily transport materials between classrooms.

Every paraprofessional needs a box of personal supplies, which may include pencils, pens, paper, markers, note cards, highlighters, a calculator, paper clips, tape, a stapler, a three-hole punch, and any other items needed throughout the day.

An accordion folder is a helpful tool to organize classroom information such as the classroom rules, lesson plans, emergency information, and specific material for individual students. It is important to have the information readily available, especially during the first few weeks, because you will refer to it frequently. Some paraprofessionals prefer to organize material into three-ring binders—one per classroom. Organization is a personal choice, but confidentiality is not, so keep student information in a secure place.

For the majority of paraprofessionals, the workday coincides with the student's school day. This makes communication with other educators difficult, but not impossible. A great deal of communication is in written format, so you will also need a pocket folder where teachers can leave notes, lessons plans, and schedule changes for you.

Entering and Exiting the Classroom

As the school year begins, the general education teacher will explain to the students that additional adults will be in the classroom at various times throughout the day. Although some paraprofessionals only work in one classroom, the majority will work in multiple settings throughout the school day. If assigned to one classroom, you will become an integral part of the classroom. When working in various classrooms throughout the day, it is likely that you will arrive while the classroom teacher is teaching—explaining an assignment, lecturing on a topic, or conducting some other type of large-group activity. It is very important to enter and exit the classroom quietly and be as inconspicuous as possible. This is not to say that students will not notice your arrival, but do not respond to this attention because it distracts from the current lesson.

Once students are accustomed to all of the extra movement, it will not be an issue for the majority of them. Nevertheless, some younger students will continue to be very excited at your arrival and unable to contain that excitement. Some students with special needs will recognize you as the person who provides the support that helps them successfully make it through a day. For these students, explain at an appropriate time the importance of focusing on the lesson and that you will attend to them as soon as the lesson finishes. Often a simple acknowledgment such as a wink will let the student know that you also are happy to see them. In the classroom, it is important to remember that you are only one of many adults who provide additional support daily.

The following are some common situations you will encounter upon your arrival:

Lecture: If you arrive in the middle of a lecture or demonstration, go directly to your workstation and read the lesson plans and notes. If certain students are not required to attend to the lecture, you will have specific instructions as to what they should do during this period. Do not leave the classroom during your scheduled time unless the classroom teacher specifically tells you that you may do so.

Cooperative groups: If you arrive and students are working in cooperative groups, find out whether students need your support. If so, help them before checking messages or talking with the classroom teacher. The majority of students will be able to participate in cooperative groups, as the roles are predetermined.

Independent or seatwork activities: If students are working at their desks, check to see if they are able to complete the work independently. If not, provide the necessary support. There will be times when the seatwork is not appropriate for a given student and that student will have an alternative assignment provided by the general or special education teacher. This time is also appropriate for reteaching and reviewing.

If the general education teacher is available to talk to you during independent activities and the students do not need support, it may be an appropriate time to discuss lessons, assignments, or questions related to specific students. Always remember the rules of confidentiality when discussing issues related to students in the classroom environment.

WORKING WITH STUDENTS

Student Expectations

It is important to remember that all students can learn and that all students should be challenged and encouraged to do their best. Expectations for students vary depending on the setting and the activity. For example, the expectations for one student in a group setting, independent activity, one-on-one activity, and the lunchroom may be different from the expectations for other students in the same classroom, but the expectations for each student should remain consistent. As the paraprofessional, you are responsible for upholding these expectations. Therefore, it is important not to let your moods affect student performance. For example, on a normal day you might overlook a behavior that, when tired, you would not tolerate. You might allow a student to put an assignment aside because you do not have the patience to deal with the activity; however, when feeling rested you would insist that the student complete the assignment. Students need to know what to expect, and when working with students, consistency is essential.

Students receive special education services because they have a disability and need support. Some conscientious adults feel that if a student is unable to finish an assignment it will reflect personally on their skills as a paraprofessional and perhaps affect the job performance evaluation. This is not the case. Not all students in the inclusive classroom are able to complete their assignments; therefore, they receive the additional support. Because of this, the work is adapted and modified to meet the students' needs. The material is at a level that will be commensurate with the students' abilities. If they are still unable to complete the assignment after modifications, the curriculum must be analyzed further and additional changes made. Therefore, it is important to hold students accountable for work completion.

At times, a student may not want your assistance when it is apparent that support is necessary. If the student refuses support and it is clear that he or she is unable to complete the assignment, several options are available. You may want to discuss the following options with your supervising teacher in advance:

Option 1: Allow the student to complete the entire assignment alone. Check the final quality of the assignment. If the quality is acceptable, the student turns in the assignment. If the student has guessed, filled in answers that have no meaning, or obviously did not understand the assignment, the student should redo the assignment. You will encounter times when a student refuses. Often the classroom teacher will need to intervene. You cannot force a student to complete the assignment. Do not get into a power struggle with the student. If the problem persists, schedule a meeting with the supervising teacher to discuss the situation. More often than not, small changes make a huge difference.

Option 2: Provide support to a small group of students instead of working one on one with a particular student. The special education paraprofessional provides consistent support only to students who have an IEP. Periodically, however, additional students from the class are included in small groups to reinforce a skill, for reteaching, or simply so the student with special needs is not consistently singled out. This is legal as long as the student does not become an integral part of the group. If a general education student consistently needs additional support, the general education teacher may choose to use the instructional modifications created for the students in special education for these struggling students also, or perhaps a referral to special education is necessary.

Option 3: On occasion, it is appropriate to change positions with the classroom teacher. From time to time, it is advantageous for the general education teacher to work with the special education students while you monitor the class during independent seatwork activities.

Establishing a Relationship

Establishing a relationship with students is important. The greater the trust, the easier it is to work with them. It is important to be friendly and take an interest in the students you work with, but it is also important to maintain the position of an adult authority figure. The boundaries established at the beginning of the relationship are important because you will encounter times when you need to be firm and discipline the students. This issue of boundaries is particularly important at the secondary level when the age difference between paraprofessionals and students may conceivably be only three or four years.

When working with students in the classroom, it is important to be accessible to them but not hover over them. At the elementary level, students frequently derive pleasure from individual assistance. As they grow and mature, some students become self-conscious and do not want to appear different. Though they may still want special assistance, fitting in with their peers becomes more important. Your major responsibility is to assist these students with special needs, but it is also important to respect, nurture, and foster independence. Therefore, if the students you support do not need assistance, walk around the classroom and help other students. You may provide support to others, but always remember that your primary area of focus is the students in special education.

Communicating With Students

Your job is to encourage students to do their best. A language of acceptance will help them feel comfortable and at ease. When working with students individually or in small groups, good eye contact is important because it indicates that you are interested in what students have to say.

When speaking to students in the classroom, address them by name. Do not use terms such as *honey, dear,* or *sport* when talking to them. Speak to students with special needs as you do to students without special needs. Do not talk down to these students, change your tone of voice, or use phrases that are not age appropriate. Students in the general education class model their behavior after yours and learn from you. If you hear students in the classroom talking down to, teasing, or bullying a student, gently correct them in private. If the problem persists, it may be necessary for the special education department to provide an inservice for the entire class.

When communicating with students, there will be times when you will need to shorten the length of sentences you use, provide directions one step at a time, or omit details. This is especially true for students with receptive language difficulties or hearing impairments. When changing the presentation method, do not change your tone of voice. Changing the manner in which the material is presented is easily done without changing your tone of voice.

TYPES OF CLASSROOM INSTRUCTION

The majority of classroom instruction takes place in a large-group, small-group, or one-on-one situation. During large-group instruction such as a class lecture, your duties may include note taking, helping students stay on task, or monitoring specific students. If a lecture is inappropriate for some students, you may provide individual support during this period. The majority of instructional support that you provide will be to individual students or small groups of students. There may be times when the classroom teacher is instructing a small group of students and your responsibility is to monitor a class activity or provide support to the general population of students. This is perfectly acceptable as long as the supervising teacher is available and physically present in the classroom.

Because the majority of your responsibilities will be with students in small groups (two to six students), the remainder of this chapter focuses on types of small-group instruction that you will encounter in the classroom environment.

This type of instruction takes place for a multitude of reasons, and understanding the purpose of the group is vital before your role can be determined. One of your primary challenges is to find ways to make instructional activities effective and efficient. Small groups can be highly effective but need to be properly organized. For a group to function well, students must possess the skills necessary to work effectively in groups.

The major advantage of a small group is that it allows students to participate on a more frequent basis and receive immediate feedback. Students also benefit from small-group instruction because it is a less threatening environment in which to ask questions and there is more opportunity to respond individually. With two adults in the classroom, small groups allow multiple activities to occur simultaneously. During small-group instruction, you may contribute by working with a group or by monitoring all of the students in the classroom while the supervising teacher works with a group. Small groups are effective for drill-and-practice activities because it is easy to monitor student response. Problem-solving and brainstorming activities are also effective when working with three or more students because students need to listen and respond to the ideas of others.

The duration of a small-group activity varies depending on the lesson or assignment. Frequently, the formation of small groups is for a specific lesson or activity and may last for only one subject block or lesson. Once the activity is complete, the composition of the groups may change for the next activity. Other small groups exist for longer periods because they convene for a long-term project or research activity. Decisions made about when to change the dynamics of the group are based on the curriculum content and lesson goals.

Not all students thrive in a small-group setting. For students to work effectively in a group, they must possess several basic skills. Students should be able to take turns and cooperate, follow directions, support one another, and analyze group performance. Often, these skills need to be monitored closely until attained. Some students need to develop the various skills before becoming part of a group. The supervising teacher will be able to provide guidelines and suggestions for teaching these skills.

Student groups fluctuate in the classroom environment depending on the predetermined objective or outcome desired by the supervising teacher. Students often are grouped in one of the following ways:

Ability levels: Students are assigned to groups according to their individual ability levels. For example, they may be grouped by reading levels: above-average readers, average readers, and students who need support with reading.

Curriculum level: Students are assigned to groups related to the type of curriculum or level of difficulty of an activity so that students work on similar skills within the group.

Individual differences: Groups are formed to allow selected students to be included with others so that they have the opportunity to learn from each other's individual differences. This grouping may also be used for students who are continually isolated from their peers.

Random grouping: Students are assigned randomly. The groups may change so that students have experience working with diverse groups of peers.

Social skill level: Groups are selected so that students can work on social skills in specific situations.

Several types of small-group instruction may occur. The most common include cooperative learning groups, mastery learning, multilevel instruction, peer tutoring, real-life learning, and the use of technology. In some of the following narratives, instructional practices, hypothetical goals, and objectives are included to help clarify the differences between the individual instructional practices. In the classroom, the general and special education teachers collaboratively develop the separate goals and objectives for students who need them. As a paraprofessional, you will help the student meet these goals.

Cooperative Learning Groups

Cooperative learning is a small-group instruction technique that allows all students to be included in the classroom with relative ease. The emphasis is on the process of learning, and the final grade is based on individual effort, group effort, and the outcome. The number of students included in each cooperative group varies depending on the unit.

Let us consider an example of cooperative learning. Imagine that a class is working on measurement during a science unit, and each group consists of four students. The students are required to measure various liquids and objects. The supervising teacher has determined the four major responsibilities in advance: gathering materials, collecting data, reading aloud, and recording the information. Please note how easily each student is able to be included (despite any student's limitations) and how students can be actively involved in this type of small group.

Gatherer: This group member gathers the material and sets up the activity. The student who has difficulty cooperating in a group situation may be assigned this task because its boundaries and limits are naturally defined.

Data collector: This group member records the specific results from the data on the group response sheet. For the student who has difficulty staying on task, this task may allow movement and keep the student actively involved in the activity. The nonreader may also be assigned this task.

Reader: This group member reads the material aloud. The student who receives support for written language may have difficulty writing but not reading. Therefore, this student could be the reader. Reading no longer interferes with the work of students who have difficulty reading because the material is read aloud by the reader, and these students obtain the material auditorily and can easily participate.

Recorder: This group member records the group response. For the student who has difficulty with reading or with written language, once these obstacles are removed the student is able to contribute his or her ideas verbally and is a fully active participant.

With cooperative groups, all students are able to participate. The student who functions at a completely different level (such as a student with mental retardation) is still able to participate while working on individual goals or objectives. With the support of the paraprofessional, the student may use this cooperative group to work on goals related to following directions, measuring, counting, and developing language.

Following directions: The student gathers the material needed for the activity. The materials may include items such as measuring cups, rulers, yardsticks, pencils, or paper. Depending on the student's ability, the directions may involve one, two, or three steps.

Measuring: If the group of students is required to measure in centimeters and millimeters, it may be appropriate for a student to first measure in inches, feet, or yards. For example, if measuring liquid, the student measures one cup of water and gives it to the group. The students use the cup of water to measure smaller quantities such as milliliters.

Counting: If the student is working on counting, he or she may count the number of rulers or yardsticks needed to measure the width of the classroom. If the student is required to put away the materials, he or she is responsible for counting the specific objects and returning them to their proper location.

Language development: The items used for the cooperative group can be tools for vocabulary development. The student can practice using the object names in sentences. Depending on the student's ability, the goal may simply be to learn the names of the students in the group.

Mastery Learning

Mastery learning is a teaching strategy used in all classrooms. It focuses on a specific skill and provides opportunities for students to gain mastery at their level through reteaching and reinforcement. With mastery learning, students often demonstrate their knowledge by completing an exam or some form of assessment (either formal or informal) at the end of the unit.

Consider the following example of mastery learning. Given 20 sentences, students must locate the noun and verb in each sentence, and they must score 80 percent or better to pass the unit.

With mastery learning, students with special needs are often able to reach the goal, although perhaps in a nontraditional way. Some students need instructional modifications or for the level of mastery to be modified. To reach the goal, many students require additional drill-and-practice exercises. This additional practice often occurs during a small-group activity or individually between the student and you or the classroom teacher.

For some students, the level of mastery is easily demonstrated by incorporating methods other than a traditional paper-and-pencil exam. Note that in the previous example, the student only needs to demonstrate knowledge of nouns and verbs. The exam for the mainstream students conceivably requires reading and writing, but the skill actually tested is whether the student is able to locate the nouns and verbs in the 20 sentences.

Many students with special needs know the purpose of nouns and verbs in a sentence. However, they are often unable to read the material, so they can partner with fluent readers or the teacher can read the test aloud. Another alternative for students who have difficulty reading is to select a 20-sentence passage at their reading level and ask them to identify the nouns and verbs from the passage.

If students have difficulty writing, test them orally. Ask them to select 10 nouns in the classroom environment, observe the actions of the other students in the class, and then state 10 verbs. Another alternative to writing is to allow students to circle or underline the correct answer if the test involves a large amount of writing.

For students with a severe discrepancy, the lesson may focus on vocabulary development using nouns and verbs. Cut out pictures from a magazine of nouns such as boy, dog, girl, or toy. Label the pictures. Add a verb to each picture, and work on sentence construction. Examples for the listed nouns may include *The boy eats, The dog plays, The girl runs,* or *The toy spins.*

Multilevel Instruction

In multilevel instruction, the supervising teacher provides the instruction to the class. With the focus placed on the key concepts, students demonstrate their knowledge through presentations, projects, or assigned activities.

Let us look at a simple example of multilevel instruction in a unit on volcanoes. The class is required to learn about the formation of volcanoes, locate active and inactive volcanoes, and learn 10 vocabulary words associated with the lesson. This is the outcome for the general population of students in the classroom.

For some students with special needs, this lesson may or may not be appropriate. Following are examples of two hypothetical students in the same classroom, Jeremy and Sarah. Jeremy is able to meet the goal with minimal modifications. Sarah, on the other hand, is performing at a level four to five years below that of her peer group. When a lesson is inappropriate for a student with special needs, the special education team develops a separate goal for the student. **Form 13, Goal Worksheet,** is a place to list individual goals and objectives.

The goal that the supervising teacher develops for Jeremy is to demonstrate how a volcano is formed, locate active and inactive volcanoes, and learn a minimum of five new vocabulary words from the class list. His goal is the same as the one for the general education students except that the number of vocabulary words is decreased. Even though the outcome is almost identical, the way Jeremy arrives at this outcome may be different.

Once the goal is set, the objectives are determined. The objectives are the steps that the student must take to meet the final goal. Let us look at the goal and objectives written for Jeremy.

Form 13: Sample Goal Worksheet

Student: Jeremy   **Subject Area:** Science

General Education Teacher: M. Smith

Special Education Teacher: L. Lee

Date: Jan. 20

Final Goal: Jeremy will demonstrate the formation of a volcano. He will learn five or more vocabulary words from the class list.

Short-Term Objectives:

Objective 1: The student is required to listen to the class lecture. He may obtain material from diagrams in supplemental textbooks.

Objective 2: The student is required to listen to the required reading on tape or join a small group and listen as material is read aloud.

Objective 3: The student will use a map to locate active and inactive volcanoes.

Objective 4: The student will create a model or diagram of a volcano in place of a paper-and-pencil test. The model will demonstrate his knowledge of the five preselected vocabulary words: volcano, vent, lava, eruption, molten rock.

As a paraprofessional, you may be required to provide support to a student like Jeremy in the classroom. Reread Objectives 1–4, and think about ways in which you may be asked to support such a student in the classroom. List your responses on a separate piece of paper, and compare them to these possible responsibilities:

- Record the textbook chapter on cassette so that Jeremy is able to listen to the chapter on tape.
- Read the chapter aloud to Jeremy, or monitor a small group of students during the reading process.

- Help find additional resource books in the library that are related to volcanoes.
- Help locate the volcanoes on a map.
- Practice using the vocabulary words in sentences.
- Provide additional drill-and-practice activities.

ACTIVITY

Materials needed: paper and pencil

In this example, Sarah is unable to complete the assignment. Sarah has mental retardation, which means that both her developmental and cognitive abilities severely lag behind those of her peer group. However, she is still able to participate in the unit even though her goal and objectives are different. Her goals and objectives could be related to vocabulary development, fine motor development, visual discrimination, or social skills. The following sample worksheet includes a goal and several objectives, which may be appropriate for a student like Sarah who performs significantly below grade level.

Form 13: Sample Goal Worksheet

Student: Sarah   **Subject Area:** Science
General Education Teacher: P. S.
Special Education Teacher: P. H.

Date: Jan. 10

Final Goal: Sarah will distinguish between a mountain, a desert, and a prairie.

Short-Term Objectives:

Objective 1: The student will look at various pictures of mountains, deserts, the ocean, and the prairie. She will be able to point to pictures of mountains. (vocabulary development and visual discrimination)

Objective 2: The student will create a book with pictures of mountains, deserts, oceans, and prairie land. She will dictate a sentence describing each geographical area. (fine motor skills and language development)

Some examples of descriptions may include the following:

A mountain is very big. Sometimes there is snow on the top. Some people go to mountains to ski.

The desert is very hot and dry. There is no grass. Cactus grows in the desert. A desert has very little rain.

The prairies are flat. Grass and flowers grow on the prairies.

The ocean is a big body of water. The water tastes salty.

Objective 3: The student will formulate sentences alone or with assistance. She may copy sentences from examples or trace over previously written sentences. (written language and fine motor skills)

Objective 4: The student will be able to distinguish between a picture of a mountain and an active volcano. (visual discrimination)

Objective 5: The student will create a model mountain out of modeling clay and share her model with the class. (social skills)

Sarah participates in the activity even though her goal and objectives are different from those of her peers.

As a paraprofessional, you may have to provide support to students like Sarah in the classroom. Reread the objectives, and think about ways in which you can support such students to meet the goal listed. Write your responses on a separate sheet of paper, and compare them to these possible responsibilities:

- Help find pictures in magazines.
- Assist with cutting, pasting, and creating a geography book.
- Find pictures of the vocabulary words.
- Practice using the vocabulary words in sentences.
- Monitor seatwork activities.
- Write the sentences dictated by the student.
- Practice several sentences verbally for the student to use in the final class presentation.

Did you write some of these on your sheet of paper? There are additional ways to support students like Sarah, but the main criterion for the objectives is that each activity relates to the goal and helps the student meet that goal.

PEER TUTORING AND LEADERSHIP OPPORTUNITIES

Peer tutoring is part of many classroom settings. Often students learn by teaching others, which can be a positive experience for both the tutor and the person receiving the tutoring. Peer tutors can lend support to students with special needs, but they must be trained so that they understand how to guide these students without completing the activity or providing answers.

Students with special needs should have the experience of being a tutor along with other leadership opportunities. Opportunities may occur in or outside of the classroom. As you discover the strengths and special talents of each student, share this information with the classroom teacher so that he or she can place the student in a tutorial or leadership role. The following are several types of tutoring activities:

- The student reads or tutors younger students, and you help the student select appropriate materials. For example, if a student has mastered basic sight words, the student could help in a primary classroom by providing drill-and-practice support.
- For the student who is unable to read fluently, a primary-level book is an option. The student can practice reading the book aloud and then read it to younger students. Students who have a developmental delay may turn the pages for a peer while the peer reads aloud.
- The student with artistic ability may demonstrate specific techniques or teach an art activity to a small group of students.
- The student who excels in math may be a math tutor.
- The student who uses specialized materials such as communication tools, Braille, or a wheelchair can demonstrate their uses to the class. Some possibilities include the following:

o Obtain a second wheelchair, and allow students to spend time in it to determine the difficulty of performing specific tasks.

o Students who are able to read Braille can provide books and teach their peers how to read them. These student can also read to the class and demonstrate how a Braillewriter works.

o Students with a communication board can demonstrate how the board functions. Following the demonstration, allow these students to teach others how to use it.

o If students use sign language, have them teach the class a sign a day and incorporate the signing techniques into the classroom.

- The student with strong verbal skills may lead a discussion group.
- If a student excels in music or the arts, provide an opportunity for a lead part in a class play or musical.
- The student who has athletic ability may be a captain of a team or lead a practice session for students who would like to increase their ability.

All students should have the opportunity to teach others. Frequently, the student with disabilities is on the receiving end, but the disability is only a small part of the student, so it is important to capitalize on the strengths and provide every student the opportunity to be a leader.

REAL-LIFE LEARNING

Real-life learning is sometimes referred to as activity-based learning. With this method, students practice and learn skills in actual or simulated settings. Examples of activity-based learning may include the following:

- teaching measurement through cooking
- teaching the concept of money by creating a class store
- providing actual job training on the site

SKILL REINFORCEMENT

Reinforcement of previously learned skills commonly occurs in small-group settings and may include preteaching material to students, providing additional drill-and-practice activities, reteaching, and reviewing materials. Small groups may also be used to support students with incomplete assignments. In a small group, it is simple to confirm individual understanding of the concept. Often, students who constantly are behind with assignments may be able to complete several assignments orally. If the purpose of an assignment is to ascertain whether students know the material, by completing assignments orally the students are able to catch up to their peer group.

ASSISTIVE TECHNOLOGY

Assistive technology is used by individuals with disabilities to perform functions that might otherwise be difficult or impossible. This technology can include mobility devices such as walkers and wheelchairs and hardware, software, and peripherals that assist in accessing computers or other information technologies. For example, students with limited hand function may use a keyboard with large keys or a special mouse to operate a computer. Students with blindness may use software that reads the text aloud in a computer-generated voice. Students with low vision often use software that enlarges screen content, allowing them to see it better. Students who are deaf may use a text telephone (TTY). Students with speech impairments may use a device that speaks aloud as they enter text via a keyboard.

Technology makes a huge difference with curriculum support for students with disabilities. Educational computer programs are terrific tools because they provide immediate feedback, which is so important for many students. Whether using the computer individually or as a class, there are programs available for all students at their current levels of performance. Many programs used for drill-and-practice activities do not allow the user to proceed until preset goals (set by the adult) are met. Computers are also appropriate for students who have trouble spelling or with fine motor skills. Word processing programs allow students to produce a quality assignment without worrying about illegible writing or misspelled words. The built in spell-checker and thesaurus are easy for students to use.

Voice recognition software supports students who have difficulty with writing or are unable to write. It allows them to speak into the computer, and the computer transcribes the material for the student. With the new voice recognition programs, students are able to program their voices in as little as one hour. Some programs are also able to scan textbook material and read it back to students.

The current technological environment is exciting because these new resources increase independence for students in the school setting and for adults in the workforce. As a paraprofessional, don't worry about whether you may be expected to work with any of these devices; you will receive training. Technology is constantly changing and new products are continually produced, so inservice training in this area tends to be ongoing.

NOTES

7

Accommodations and Modifications

If there is anything a man can do well, I say let him do. Give him a chance.

Abraham Lincoln

The first six chapters of this book make little distinction between accommodations and modifications. Simply put, both are changes to the curriculum, instructional techniques, or the environment. And special education students are not the only students who require accommodations and modifications. A number of students receive supplemental support and accommodations under Title I, English as a second language, and 504 Plans, which are separate programs outside of special education.

WHAT IS THE DIFFERENCE?

By now you are probably wondering, "So what is the difference between an accommodation and a modification? Both involve a change for students." This is true—both do involve a change. The difference between the two is in the outcome (result). With an accommodation, the outcome is the same for all students, but some arrive at it in a slightly different way. Modifications are different from accommodations because they involve a change in the content that often results in a different outcome.

Accommodations

It is lunchtime for Mary and John's class. Both students are in line and ready to go. Mary walks, and John uses a wheelchair. In this scenario, both arrive to the lunchroom, but in different ways. The wheelchair is an accommodation for John. Let us look at another example, this time related to vision. Mary and John return to class after lunch. It's math time, and the students are required to copy some problems from the board. John has good vision, and Mary has extreme myopia. John is able to sit anywhere in the classroom because he is able to see the board. Mary, on the other hand, uses glasses and although the glasses allow her to see better, she still has low vision. So she has a special seat two feet from the board, which she uses when required to copy from the board. In this scenario, Mary's glasses and the location of her desk are accommodations. No one would consider taking away John's wheelchair, depriving Mary of her glasses, or requiring her to sit at the back of the class. Why? Because these simple changes allow the students to be independent.

Accommodations in the classroom occur on a regular basis for all students. Many accommodations are simply best teaching practice. Teachers often make them without thinking about it. Very simply put, teachers monitor and adjust instruction, assignments, or the environment to meet the needs of the students.

The following list includes various types of accommodations used in the classroom environment. The type of accommodation is listed in parentheses following the example. As you will notice, the outcome for the student remains the same, but the manner in which it is achieved is different. These examples demonstrate changes in the pace, presentation, environment, assessment, assignment, grading, reinforcement, and follow-through support:

- The class has been working on an assignment, and the allotted time is over. The teacher notes that the majority of the students have not finished, therefore he allows additional time to complete the assignment. (Change in the pace of the assignment)
- The teacher is lecturing, and she continually monitors the students' response. While scanning the class, she notices that a majority of the students look confused. She takes a blank transparency and begins to draw a diagram to explain the lesson. (Change in the presentation of material from auditory to visual)
- The students are boisterous, and several groups of students must be separated. The teacher rearranges the desks in the classroom and assigns all students to a new seat. (Change in the environment)
- A student is unable to complete an assignment in a written format, so the teacher allows the student to create a project in lieu of a written report. (Change of assignment)
- The paraprofessional reads the test aloud to a student who is unable to read it alone. The student verbally gives the answer, and the paraprofessional writes the answer on the test. (Change in support and follow-through)
- A student receives a study guide from the teacher to help prepare for the test at home. (Change in the method of support)
- A volatile student is allowed to leave the classroom when he becomes emotionally upset. He goes to a quiet area outside of the classroom. (Change in the environment; change in reinforcement)
- A student's support from the paraprofessional includes breaking the assignment into smaller parts and providing oral clues to redirect the student with seatwork. (Change of assignment)

Modifications

Modifications involve presentation, materials, grading, and assessments, and the outcome for the student is different from that of the peer group. Modifications are more restricted, and the supervising teacher determines which type to use.

As a paraprofessional, frequently you will carry out modifications under the direction of the supervising teacher. In the following list, the type of modification is listed in parentheses following the example:

- A student is unable to understand the information in the social studies textbook, so the special education teacher provides specialized curriculum. (Change in the curriculum)
- On the weekly spelling test, a student's list is modified to 6 words instead of the regular list of 12 words. The student's grade is based on the percentage of words spelled correctly. (Change of assignment; change of grading)
- A student is required to complete only the even-numbered problems on the math assignment. (Change of assignment)
- During science, Jonathan's responsibility is to gather and put away the materials needed for the science experiment. When giving an item to each student in the group, Jonathan addresses the student by name. If he does not remember the student's name, he will ask, "What is your name?" and then address the student using his or her name. (Change of material and assignment)

As noted, there is a difference between accommodations and modifications. As a paraprofessional, you can implement accommodations. The supervising teacher provides the modifications to you to implement. This is an integral part of your job because these changes will assist students in their daily work. Instructional changes include adapting the material so that a student is better able to understand and/or complete the assignment, reading a test to a student, or providing additional support for a specific project or in a specific subject area. There will be times when a student needs an instructional modification to complete an assignment and other times when the student is able to complete the assignment alone. Therefore, instructional accommodations and modifications are continually readjusted to meet the needs of the student.

Curricular modifications are different from instructional ones because they include concrete changes to the actual curriculum and are determined in advance by the special education team. When a curricular modification is developed, the student may have an assignment that is very different from that of the rest of the class. The outcome for this student may or may not be the same as that of the peer group.

Because not all situations can be anticipated, there may be on-the-spot instructional modifications and accommodations in response to an activity that is about to occur. Let us look at a hypothetical situation:

Melissa is frustrated and struggling with the reading level of the science textbook. Your instructions are to allow her to read the material independently and help her answer the questions at the end of the chapter. You note that she is becoming increasingly frustrated, so you quietly approach her and ask if she would like your help reading the unfamiliar words. While helping her, you notice that when the material is read aloud, she grasps the main idea quickly. Therefore, it seems that the main interference is the textbook reading level and not the actual content of the material. You decide to read the chapter aloud even though it is not one of the accommodations listed for Melissa. With the additional reading support, she is able to complete the assignment and answer the discussion questions.

This is considered an on-the-spot accommodation for the student. As a paraprofessional, you have to determine whether to help the student with the assignment or allow the student to struggle and help with only the chapter questions. In this short example, it is difficult to determine whether the student needs a little support with the reading or whether the curriculum is becoming too difficult. Thus, it is important to document this information and share it with the supervising teacher. When documenting, you will need to ascertain (to the best of your ability) why the student was experiencing difficulty with the reading. Is the reading level too difficult? What type of mistake occurred? Is the student unable to sound out new vocabulary introduced in the text? What results occurred when the material was read aloud? Was the student able to answer questions at the end of the chapter when the material was read aloud? The following sample of **Form 14, Instructional Changes,** may be used to report this information, which helps the supervising teacher plan upcoming lessons more efficiently and helps determine whether future curriculum needs to be modified to meet the individual student's needs.

Form 14: Sample Instructional Changes

Date: May 19

Student: Susan L.

Subject Area: Science

Area of Difficulty (explain this specifically and objectively)	Change Implemented	Result
Science textbook. Reading level was too difficult. Student was unable to sound out unfamiliar words and was struggling with the reading. When reading alone, she was unable to answer the questions.	First, I helped the student figure out the unfamiliar words. Because she was frustrated and behind in her work, I read the second part of the textbook aloud to her.	The student was able to answer the questions at the end of the chapter without searching for the answers.

When working with students, you may also encounter times when it is necessary to deviate from the planned lesson instead of making an on-the-spot modification. The termination of an assignment may occur because a student has not acquired the basic skills to complete the assignment, completes part of the assignment but it is completely wrong, is too distressed to complete the assignment, or refuses to do the activity. Because it is the responsibility of the supervising teacher to develop the lesson and provide the materials, it is not appropriate for you as the paraprofessional to create new activities or redesign individual lessons. If a student does not have the basic skills to complete an assignment, you need to contact the supervising teacher before continuing with the lesson.

You may also encounter times when the classroom teacher prefers not to make a decision regarding the curriculum and would like the response to come from the special education team. Because the special education teacher may not be available on short notice, what should be done? It is important to have an alternate plan in place so that valuable learning time is not lost. To prepare for this situation, alternative work folders are often created. The folders may include previous incomplete assignments, drill-and-practice activities for previously learned skills, educational games or activities, review activities, or homework. The material in the work folder can also be used when a student completes an assignment before the allotted lesson time is over. It is important to note that some students are very adept at finding ways to delay a lesson with the intention of avoiding it altogether. Therefore, when terminating a lesson, document the reason and contact the special education teacher so that adjustments are made prior to subsequent lessons.

Now let us look at another example of deviating from the original lesson plan:

> The students are preparing for a social studies group project. Each student is assigned a specific job in the cooperative group. As they gather the materials, the fire alarm sounds, which of course disrupts the preplanned activity. When the students return to the classroom, there is not enough time to complete the project, so the teacher decides to use the remaining class period for silent reading. Scott (a student you support) does not have a book suitable for independent reading. Because you do not want to lose valuable learning time, a suitable activity must be determined. Several options come to mind. In his personal work folder, you notice vocabulary flashcards intended to reinforce the vocabulary after the social studies activity. After a quick glance, you decide that the cards could be used to preview the vocabulary instead. You note that Scott has a book for silent reading time, but it is too difficult for him to read alone, so you could also offer to read the book aloud. Scott also has a work folder filled with make-up work and several assignments that need corrections. Because all three activities seem appropriate, you decide to ask Scott which he would prefer to do for the remaining 20 minutes of class.

This situation requires an on-the-spot change from the normal class activity. The vocabulary cards, although developed for review, could easily be used for preview. Making corrections to the assignments in the work folder also is an appropriate choice. Because the other students are reading silently, it would also be acceptable to find a quiet area and read his book aloud to him. In this example, the paraprofessional can easily make a decision and select an appropriate activity. The only follow-up needed in this situation is to contact the supervising teacher and determine an appropriate book so that Scott has one available for the next silent reading block.

LEVELS OF CHANGE

The changes that occur in the classroom can be grouped into categories. Keep in mind when reading about the following that there is overlap. From the most common to the most complex, these changes include reinforcing the content area, adapting the content area, developing an alternative curriculum, and developing parallel activities.

Reinforcing the Content Area

Reinforcement usually falls into the category of accommodations. Often, reinforcing the general education curriculum allows the student to complete the required assignments either alone, with support, or with some instructional modifications. As a paraprofessional, you will be responsible for carrying out many of these accommodations and modifications daily.

The most common instructional accommodation is reinforcement of the content area. Frequently, this reinforcement is implemented with individual students or in a small-group setting. A small amount of additional reinforcement is often all the support a student may need to complete assignments and fulfill the class requirements. Supplemental aids such as study guides, outlines, or audiocassettes are also used as reinforcement tools. Reinforcing the content area includes previewing, preteaching, and reteaching.

Previewing material means that you look through the material with the student before it is presented. Discuss boldfaced vocabulary words and their meanings. Read the captions, and discuss the subject headings. Read the end-of-unit comprehension questions so that the student knows what to look for when reading. Ask the student to recall as much information as possible about the specific topic so that the new concepts can be associated with previously learned knowledge.

Preteaching material helps the student understand the concept before it is presented in the class. For example, if the upcoming lesson is related to prepositions, you may provide the student with simple examples of prepositions and ask the student to use them in sentences. In social studies, science, or reading, discuss the vocabulary in the context of the curriculum. Develop background information before reading.

Reteaching material takes place after the lesson has been presented. At times, classroom instruction and guided practice sessions do not provide sufficient practice for a student with special needs. As you work through assignments individually, you will be able to determine if the student missed a step in a process and, perhaps, to identify the specific type of error that is causing difficulty.

Adapting the Content Area

It is the responsibility of the special education team to determine whether or when curriculum modifications should be implemented. Modifying or changing the actual curriculum is not the responsibility of the paraprofessional. Therefore, in this category the team will make the actual changes to the curriculum. You, in turn, may be responsible for implementing the instructional modifications to the adapted material.

When adapting the content area, the team may decide that some assignments should be shortened, others may be completed in a small group with assistance, and in some cases that the student is not required to complete the assignment at all. In the area of spelling, the student may be required to learn a modified list of words and spend the week completing drill-and-practice activities in place of the required classroom activities. The student may dictate answers to a modified list of questions, and someone may write them for the student. Certain assignments may be completed orally to check for comprehension instead of having to give the answers in a written format.

Developing an Alternative Curriculum

In this category, supplemental materials and activities may be provided to the student. The supplemental materials may have similar content to the general education curriculum but contain a limited vocabulary or have a lower readability level. The supervising teacher provides the materials.

Developing Parallel Activities

For some students, the outcome of the lesson or activity may be completely different, even though they may perform the same type of activity as their peers. For example, a student with a parallel curriculum may be required to listen to a story on tape while the rest of the students in the class are required to read the material alone. When unaware of the student's individualized education plan (IEP) goal, it may appear to others that the student is not actively involved in the classroom activity. But the goal for this student may be to listen quietly for a predetermined amount of time and raise his or her hand when called on. In reality, the final goal for the student may be a socialization goal instead of an academic goal. A student with a fine motor goal may work on letter formation, use templates, or create objects with clay while his or her peers write a story. The student with a parallel math curriculum may use the calculator to perform basic math operations while the rest of the students in class perform advanced calculations. In this case, the student's goal may be to learn and use the functions of the calculator. Often, students with a parallel curriculum have functional IEP goals, which are often based on the skills a student will need to live independently as an adult in a supervised apartment or a group home.

GETTING ORGANIZED

The Resources include a collection of forms that can be used to document the accommodations and modifications listed in a student's IEP. **Form 15, Curriculum,** provides space to provide a narrative of the student's strengths, and modifications can be listed in nine different areas. Form 15 is appropriate for a student who requires more intense support throughout the school day. **Form 16, Textbooks, Form 17, Daily Assignments**, and **Form 18, Assessments,** list common modifications and accommodations in easy-to-use checklists. The checklists, completed in conjunction with the supervising teacher, are handy reference tools. If you work with several students in one classroom, it is easy to confuse which students receive what specific services. Once these checklists are complete, the supervising teacher determines whether copies should be distributed to all team members. In some situations, the supervising teacher provides a list of the instructional changes. If you receive such a list, be sure to clarify the procedures and expectations before working with the student. If a form contains personal reminders and notes, do not make copies to distribute unless you have permission from a certified team member.

Organization of Material

During the course of the school year, you may develop supplemental materials for students. It is important to file and save the materials you create. Materials such as vocabulary and spelling flashcards are easy to make and store, and will be used until a new curriculum is adopted by the school district. Some materials are more time-consuming to create. For example, a student may need a special audiocassette such as a paraphrased version, which highlights only the most important information in the textbook, or possibly an audiocassette that corresponds to a specific study guide. Customized audiocassettes take time to create. Often, audio versions of the classroom textbooks and novels are available for purchase directly from the publisher, but you have to determine whether the school's budget allows such purchases. Cataloging and saving the material takes additional time, but doing so will save time in the future because the material can be reused. This section includes some ways to save and store material for future reference.

Often materials are saved in four-inch three-ring binders. Label each binder with the subject and grade level. Insert pocket folders or clear transparency holders, and label and insert tabs to identify each unit. As supplemental materials are created, insert the material into the corresponding pocket. Each year, material can be added to the binder. In addition, index cards can easily be stored in small recipe boxes. Label each recipe box with the subject area, such as Grade 3 Spelling Words, Grade 8 Social Studies Vocabulary with Definitions, or Dolch Sight Words.

What should be saved? The answer is simple. Save everything that may be used for review or with additional students in the future. Materials may include the following:

- index cards with vocabulary words on the front and definitions on the back, spelling and sight word drill-and-practice cards, and boldfaced words from textbooks
- individual audiocassettes of textbooks or novels
- discussion questions (with answers) for units, with page numbers and location clues if available
- study guides, teacher-created units, and corresponding assessments and supplemental materials used to reinforce the unit
- worksheets and supplemental materials used for games and related activities created to reinforce skills

Educators and paraprofessionals often make additional copies of the adapted material to store in a central location so that all educators may access the material. The central storage is often located in the district special education office. When copies of audiocassettes, assessments, and units of study are stored in a central location, individual teachers can make copies or check out the audiocassettes, if needed.

FREQUENTLY ASKED QUESTIONS

It is common for questions related to instructional modifications to arise. Frequently, the questions are specific, and it is difficult to provide an answer because the response will vary depending on the student, the classroom, and the supervising teacher. The following are some of the most frequently asked questions related to working in the classroom:

Is it okay to work with students who are not special education students? At times you may review a lesson, provide drill-and-practice activities, or reinforce a specific skill that would benefit general education students as well. Therefore, you may be asked to include additional students in your group. This is perfectly acceptable as long as the students do not become a permanent part of the special education group. Guidelines for working with general education students are provided by the general education teacher, not the special education teacher.

How do I know if the activity has been adjusted too much or too little? You may sometimes question how much or how little instructional support to provide for a student. For example, you may wonder whether you should read an entire passage aloud or help the student only with the difficult words. Use your best judgment, and then increase or decrease the amount of support. The longer you work with the student, the more skilled you will become in making such determinations.

What do I do if the student is unable to complete the assignment even with prompts and support? It is appropriate for you to guide the student and provide support, but you should never complete the assignment for the student. If the student is unable to complete the work, it may be an indicator that the work is still too difficult. Make note of your concerns to discuss with the supervising teacher. If the student is unable to complete the assignment, put it aside and talk to the supervising teacher before the next class session.

The student seems to be able to do the work independently, so what should I do during the class period? Step back, allow the student to complete the work, and spot-check it periodically for accuracy. It is important for the student to recognize that support is available if needed, but it is also very important to encourage and foster independence. Therefore, do not hover over the student if he or she is able to do the work independently. Instead, use the time to walk around the class and help others who may need some assistance.

I do not feel comfortable in some classrooms because I do not know the subject material. What should I do? Often, you will work across grade levels and curriculum areas. You are not expected to be an expert in every field. If you are not familiar with the material, you may read specific chapters and access the teacher's guide so that you can preview the unit before it is taught. When working with a student in an area such as mathematics, you may want to review skills before trying to help the student. Often you will be in the classroom for the instruction component, so you will be able to learn right along with the students.

NOTES

8

Helping All Students Learn

There is a brilliant child locked inside every student.

Marva Collins

Because all students are unique, a successful strategy for one student may not be applicable for another. Therefore, the remainder of this book provides a potpourri of ideas to use in the classroom. The ideas are grouped by category and numbered for quick and easy reference.

Many students with special needs encounter difficulty in the area of reading. Because reading encompasses a major part of each school day, textbook modifications are critical if the student is to experience success throughout the school day. (For specific examples for working with students during a reading class, see Chapter 10.) This chapter discusses general modifications that can be used for all students at all levels and are applicable for most textbooks.

PREREADING STAGE

You may encounter students with a large discrepancy between their individual ability and that of their peers. If a student is unable to read or write, many of the activities listed in this section are inappropriate. Prewriting strategies that are appropriate for these students are listed in Chapter 11, and they include activities for the introduction of letters and sound–symbol relationships as well as some basic suggestions.

For nonreaders, an optional prereading program is *Phonemic Awareness: Ready-to-Use Lessons, Activities, and Games* (Scott, 1999). The scripted 20-minute lessons are appropriate for individuals or small groups of students who are nonreaders. Phonemic awareness training may be used as a prerequisite to reading or for elementary students who have not had success with traditional reading programs. The training video *Phonemic Awareness: The Sounds of Reading* (Scott, 2000) demonstrates how to teach phonemic awareness and apply the principles of the program in the classroom.

CREATING AUDIOTAPES

Audiotapes are a valuable tool for students. Students who experience difficulty reading may use them during the school day and take them home to review materials for upcoming tests. Not only are tapes valuable to students with special needs, but they also provide support to students who have been absent from class. Often, tapes can be purchased directly from the textbook publishers. If they are not available, they can be created. If you are asked to make tapes, it can be an advantage for you because doing so provides a way to get a comprehensive overview of the curriculum.

The supervising teacher determines the format that best meets the needs of individual students. If study guidelines, comprehension checkpoints, vocabulary, and other pertinent information are required for the tapes, the supervising teacher provides this information to you. Before creating tapes, consider the following suggestions:

1. Select a high-quality tape for the original recording. Label the original, and store it in a safe place. Less expensive tapes may be used for copies because students frequently lose them.

2. When preparing tapes, read in a clear voice. Find a quiet place with no distractions. Record several minutes of silence and then listen to the recording. Is the recorder picking up background noise? If background noises such as doors closing, telephones ringing, or conversations are apparent, change location.

3. Textbook material should be read at approximately 120–175 words per minute. Practice by selecting a passage of approximately 150 words. Read the passage several times while using a timer to calculate your reading speed. When you have finished, listen to the recording. Make sure that it is clear and easily understood. This is not as easy as it seems. A good recording is difficult to create.

4. Begin the recording with a statement of the title, chapters, and page numbers recorded (e.g., "Grade 3—Social Studies—Chapter 1, pages 7–18"). Label the tape. The labeling system should be consistent for each tape to simplify filing. It is important to have a duplicate copy in case of loss. These tapes will be used in the upcoming years.

5. Often, a list of study guidelines is recorded at the beginning of the tape. This helps orient the student to the main points of the section. The guidelines may include the key vocabulary words listed in bold type and the study questions located at the end of each unit. If there is a written study guide for the unit, file it with the tape.

6. Comprehension checkpoints such as "Please stop the tape here, and list three uses of water" may be recorded on the tape. If this format is used, a study guide can be provided to the student with the corresponding checkpoints and answers. Another option is to record the questions and then pause, allowing the student to answer, and then record the answer. This provides immediate feedback for the student. The supervising

teacher provides the objectives of the lesson and will help determine where the specific checkpoints should be located.

7. Ask whether an extra textbook is available for special education students. On the inside front cover, place an index card with the key symbols that relate to specific portions of the tape. For example:

- An asterisk (*) may indicate a portion of the text that has been paraphrased on the recording.
- The number sign (#) may indicate that the student should stop and give the definition for a word in bold type.

The special education and general education teachers determine the symbols to be used on the book key.

8. If a student is required to read the material alone, alternate pages of the textbook may be recorded. This allows the student to listen to one page and read one page either silently or aloud. Be sure to note on the tape's label that the recording contains only alternate pages. This technique helps students who are able to read but struggle to keep up with day-to-day reading.

9. Paraphrase the entire text, with simplified vocabulary for students who are unable to read. The supervising teacher provides the main objectives of the lesson. When paraphrasing, include only the most important material. Talk about the pictures, bold print, and diagrams. Paraphrasing is difficult, so practice before attempting to record the material.

PREVIEWING OR PRETEACHING MATERIALS

Materials can also be previewed with students, which helps them acquire a basic understanding of the concept before it is presented in the classroom.

10. Create an audiotape of the assignment. Allow the student to take the tape home before the material is read in class. If the student is familiar with the main characters, story, and plot, it will be easier to understand the material when presented by the general education teacher.

11. Preview and discuss pictures in textbooks before material is read in class. Ask the student to tell you as much as possible about the subject. Build on the student's background knowledge. For example, if the story is about crossing the Atlantic Ocean on a ship, ask the student what he or she knows about ships and oceans. How does an ocean look, sound, feel, smell, and taste? Has the student ever been on a ship? If so, what did it feel like, what did he or she see, hear, taste, or touch? Try to relate new concepts to previous experiences, and build on the student's prior knowledge whenever possible.

12. When the student receives a new book, discuss the publisher's organizational strategies. Check for understanding on how to use the following components: table of contents, index, chapter summaries, glossary, and appendixes. Also, point out the use of bold type, captions, and images. Students often need instruction on how to use the

subject index; do not take for granted that students know how to do this. Students with disabilities have gaps in learning. The more the gaps are filled, the easier it is for students to learn.

13. Review the bold words from the reading material, and practice reading them. Define and discuss the vocabulary in the context of the unit. Practice using the words in sentences directly related to the textbook material. It is important to have a teacher's guide or student book so that words with multiple meanings are defined within the context of the unit. For example, assume that you have a list of vocabulary words without specific definitions. The list includes the words *bluff, stern,* and *bear.* Which definition would you use?

Word	Definition 1	Definition 2
bluff	steep bank or cliff	to fool; to mislead
stern	rear part of a ship	harsh; strict
bear	large animal	to support; to carry

Now assume that the student has told you the topic is early explorers. Look at the words and their definitions in the previous chart. What definition should be taught? Even when the subject is defined, it is difficult to select the correct meaning without a teacher's guide.

14. Provide the student with a list of discussion questions before the student reads the text. Skim the material, and help the student locate the answers by including the page numbers and clues with discussion questions.

15. Ask the general or special education teacher for a student textbook in which to write. Highlight important information in it, and color-code it. An example follows:

Color Key (*taped into the front of the textbook*)
yellow—vocabulary words
blue—definitions
green—topic sentences, important facts, and test information

16. Generate a list of new vocabulary words, and provide an outline of the main ideas for each unit. The student can use this as a take-home study guide.

17. In some classrooms, students are required to read the material aloud. If reading aloud during class causes anxiety for the student, select several paragraphs from the unit to practice. Provide the list with the specific paragraphs to the supervising teacher. Later, if the student is required to read aloud, he or she is prepared.

18. After reading a paragraph or section of a textbook, ask the student to paraphrase the material. Paraphrasing will help the student recall the material because it involves restating the main ideas using his or her own vocabulary. The RAP acronym that follows will help the student remember the three steps involved:

Read the paragraph.
Ask yourself to recall the main idea and several details about the material.
Practice saying the main ideas and important details in your own words.

19. Summarization is an important technique to help students recall information. It may be verbal or written depending on the student's skill level. When reading aloud, stop after key paragraphs or sections. Ask the student to summarize the information. When the student is reading alone, ask him or her to write two to three sentences to summarize the section. Each time a student stops to process, it aids retention. In this case, the student reads and speaks, or reads and writes. For some students, all three steps may be appropriate. Read the information, verbalize it, and write it.

20. Ask the supervising teacher for an additional set of textbooks for the student to keep at home for personal use. Students with disabilities often have more homework than the average student, sometimes in every subject, and it is difficult to carry every textbook home daily.

ON-THE-SPOT CHANGES

You may not always have an opportunity to preview materials with students in advance. The following strategies will assist students with the material in the classroom setting during the actual lesson:

21. Read the text aloud using a guided reading procedure. With this method, which is appropriate for a small group of struggling readers, the students are guided systematically through the material. As you read the material aloud, stop frequently to ask questions, summarize, and paraphrase the information, and ask questions to check for understanding.

22. At times, the class may be divided into two separate groups. (Small groups allow students to participate more frequently.) The students with special needs may be divided among them or remain in one group. It is important to have a copy of the discussion questions so that both groups discuss the same information.

23. As students read aloud, allow the student who has trouble with reading to "pass or play" when his or her turn arrives because the student may not be comfortable reading in front of a large group. As the comfort level increases, the student will take more risks. If the student is required to read aloud, strategically seat him or her near someone who is able to help decode any unknown words.

24. When working with small groups, choral reading allows all students to participate. With choral reading, the students read aloud with you. It helps them develop read-aloud skills, learn basic sight words, and increase fluency. Choral reading works best with small passages.

25. Cloze reading is another read-aloud strategy that keeps all students actively involved. With a cloze reading procedure, you read aloud and randomly stop at various points, which is when the students fill in the missing words. For example:

Sam and Isaac were off to play in a baseball tournament. When they arrived at the baseball _____ (field), the teams were lined up and the _____ (tournament) was ready to begin.

26. Buddy reading allows two students in your group to read together while you monitor them. Students can take turns reading sentences, one student can read while the other listens, or one reads and the other rereads.

27. Provide an outline of the textbook material for the student, and allow the student to take notes on the outline while peers read aloud.

28. Supplemental materials may be available in a high-interest, low-vocabulary format. These are often listed in the teacher's guide under a heading such as "supplementary resources."

29. It is often appropriate to make an audio recording of material while it is read aloud during class. This is a time-saver because the material and the class discussion are recorded for future use. This also supports any student who is absent.

30. Prepare an outline of important material for the student to use as a guide when listening to materials.

NOVELS, FREE-CHOICE, AND SILENT READING

Many classrooms have a silent reading block incorporated into the daily class schedule. At the secondary level, entire class periods may be devoted to reading material in class. For students with special needs, this time should also be productive, especially if they need assistance and support is not available for the entire class period. If a student with special needs is unable to read the material alone, he or she will sometimes pretend to read the material. When this happens, the class period is often wasted, and the student usually ends up completing the assignment at home.

31. Ask students to make audio recordings of their favorite books and novels, which may be placed in a classroom library or the media center for other students to check out. These taped books are an alternative for students during silent reading time. At the secondary level, students may also record required classroom novels for classroom libraries.

32. If there is a nonreader in the class, read aloud to a small group of students. Vary the students in the group, and allow them to choose a friend to participate in the group.

33. Check the school or local library for movie versions of current class novels or stories. A small group of students may view the video instead of reading the material. Students may then compare and contrast the storylines of the book and the video.

34. When assistance is not available, the general education teacher may appoint a student to be teacher for a day. This student can read the material aloud to a small group or to an individual student. Use a checklist such as **Form 19, Volunteer List,** to record the names of volunteers. Give all students the opportunity to be teacher for a day.

35. Provide opportunities for students to read, read, and read more. Expose struggling readers to as much print material as possible, and encourage students to read at their level. Look for books with larger print and fewer words per page. Magazines and comic books are also options.

TRACKING DIFFICULTIES

Students frequently have difficulty following along during read-aloud activities. For some students, the reading level of the classroom textbook is too difficult, so it may be easier for them to listen and obtain the information auditorily. For other students, directionality has not been established; they may not be sure where to begin reading, try to read from right to left, or have difficulty moving from line to line. These students may continually lose their place, and you may feel as though you are continually redirecting them. If this occurs, they are probably having trouble with visual tracking.

36. Partner the student with a peer so that they may share the textbooks. The peer can guide the student who is having difficulty.

37. Provide oral location clues when reading aloud. Redirect the student by pointing out page and paragraph numbers frequently. For example, "Please begin reading on page 54, paragraph 2."

38. During read-aloud time, frequently check to see if the student is in the correct place. If you are not available, the student should be paired with another student or seated near the general education teacher so that tracking can be easily monitored.

39. A bookmark will help the student keep his or her place while reading and can easily be moved from one line to the next, helping the student who would otherwise skip lines while reading.

40. Draw a horizontal arrow running from left to right on an index card. This will help the student with directionality.

41. Cut a window into an index card to help the student focus on one line of text at a time. Because all books have a different font size, the student will need one custom-made card per textbook. Here is an example of a window card for this book:

custom-made card per textbook. Here is an example of a window card for this book:

42. Make a picture frame cutout from construction paper. The student will be able to see several lines of print, yet block out the distracting stimuli. The picture frame is larger than the window in the card from #41 (and may be as large as a full page), allowing the student to see more of the page. Experiment with various sizes to see which provides the most benefit to the student. Here is an example:

42. Make a picture frame cutout from construction paper. The student will be able to see several lines of print, yet block out the distracting stimuli. The picture frame is larger than the window in the card from #41 (and may be as large as a full page), allowing the student to see more of the page. Experiment with various sizes to see which provides the most benefit to the student. Here is an example:

43. Allow the student to listen to the material and view the pictures while someone else reads aloud.

STUDENTS WITH HEARING IMPAIRMENTS

The following suggestions provide additional support for the student with a hearing impairment:

44. The student should be seated near the teacher.

45. Use visual signals frequently to secure the student's attention when reading aloud. Redirect as necessary.

46. Speak and read clearly, in a normal tone, and at a moderate pace.

47. Rephrase the content areas when reviewing lectures.

48. Do not provide lengthy explanations.

49. Provide an outline and a vocabulary list in written format before introducing new material. Practice reading the words aloud. Encourage the student to preview the information at home before the lesson is presented in class.

50. Present new vocabulary words in sentences instead of in isolation. Many words look similar to lip readers.

51. If the student seems confused with verbal directions, repeat and summarize the information or provide a written copy.

52. If the student reads lips, a swivel chair is beneficial. The student will be able to see the teacher and the interpreter at all times.

53. If a student uses hearing devices and seems to be having difficulty, contact the hearing specialist. Hearing aids often need to be tested and adjusted.

STUDENTS WITH VISION IMPAIRMENTS

If a student with vision impairments appears to be inattentive and looking around the classroom, the student may be relying on the auditory channel to obtain information. Students with vision impairments often experience visual fatigue during classroom assignments and may need to rest their eyes.

Various materials are available specifically for visually impaired students. The vision consultant may order enlarged-font textbooks, magnifiers, closed-circuit television, and computer software with large fonts and pictures. If the student is required to use special technology, you will receive instructions about how to use the equipment. This training is very important because it enables you to assist the student when the specialist is not available.

54. Provide audiotapes for the student's use. If the recordings are made in house, they should be recorded on tape players with variable recording speeds, enabling the student to increase the speed as auditory skills are refined.

55. Allow extra time for the student to complete assignments. Be aware of visual fatigue during classroom activities. Some signs of visual fatigue are red eyes, rubbing the eyes, laying the head on the desk, and squinting. Discuss with the supervising teacher the types of modifications that should be implemented if the student experiences extreme visual fatigue. One possibility is to allow some of the assignments to be completed orally. If you choose this method, write a note on the blank assignment page indicating that it was completed orally, and then initial and date it. The general education teacher or parent can contact you should questions arise.

56. When directing questions to a student with a vision impairment, address the student by name. Often students with vision impairments do not respond to body language, gestures, and/or subtle visual clues due to their low vision.

57. Make audio recordings of daily assignments. The student may listen to them as many times as needed. This is simple to do and it fosters independence.

58. Touch is important for visually impaired students. Provide hands-on experiences whenever possible.

NOTES

9

Support Across the Curriculum

Children are like wet cement. Whatever falls on them will leave an impression.

Haim Ginott

Students qualify for special education services in specific academic areas, so support is often provided in those isolated areas of the curriculum. If a student has difficulty reading, support is required during the reading block. However, what happens with the student's program for the remainder of the school day? Is the student only required to read during the reading block? Of course not; reading impacts the entire school day. A student who has difficulty writing usually receives support during a written language block, but what happens when the student is required to take notes during a history lecture? Some students who have difficulty processing information receive support from a language specialist. The small amount of service helps with some academics, but what about class lectures and the instructions given throughout the school day?

Support across the curriculum varies. Some areas that are problematic for students are daily assignments, organization, accessing information presented orally, and following directions. Although it is neither possible nor healthy for students to receive support the entire school day, it is important to be aware of these areas and to discuss with students how to apply the new skills learned throughout the school day.

DAILY ASSIGNMENTS

The principle purpose of a daily assignment is to verify students' understanding of a concept or to practice a newly acquired skill. More often than not, students are asked to demonstrate their understanding in a written format. For typical students, this is generally a simple task. They are able to complete the assignment quickly and move on to other projects or perhaps get a head start on daily homework assignments. This is not always true for students with special needs. Although many students with learning disabilities have average to above-average intelligence, some may require additional time to complete an assignment due to the reading level or the written language skills required. Student who need additional time to complete assignments frequently fall behind and spend a large portion of the school day trying to catch up to the other students. Students with special needs regularly fall into this group because there simply is not enough time during the class period to complete the assignments.

The first step in accommodating the curriculum is to determine the assignment objective. This is one reason why it is important for you as the paraprofessional to be in the classroom when the directions for assignments are given. Once the objective is determined, changes can be made accordingly. For the student who is consistently behind and unable to catch up during the allotted class time, it is often appropriate to modify the assignment.

ACTIVITIES

Activity 1: The classroom teacher has assigned 30 double-digit multiplication problems. The assignment includes copying the math problems from the student textbook onto paper. Upon arrival, you note that the student has copied and completed 14 problems, but many are incorrect. After closer examination, you note that the student has transposed many numbers during the copying process. Could this be the reason that the answers are incorrect? After checking the student's answers with a calculator, you see that all of the answers are correct. The student's criterion is 80 percent mastery, but he has achieved 100 percent. In this scenario, is it necessary for the student to complete all 30 problems when he has demonstrated that the first 14 are correct? Probably not, considering that the objective of the lesson was to demonstrate knowledge of double-digit multiplication.

This scenario demonstrates the importance of carefully analyzing a multistep problem to determine the reason(s) for errors. In this case, the error was a result of transposing numbers when copying from the book. Take a moment to list the possible errors a student may encounter when copying a double-digit multiplication problem from the board or textbook. For each error, list an accommodation that could help the student.

Error	Accommodation

The following chart lists some of the possible errors along with potential ways to support the student. Did you include some of these on your list?

Error	*Accommodation*
Copying errors	Provide a hard copy for the student to write on so he or she does not have to copy the problems. Copy the problems from the board, and give them to the student.
Incorrect alignment	Provide graph paper. Turn the student's notebook sideways so the vertical lines form natural columns.
Calculation errors	Provide a multiplication table or a calculator so the student can verify the calculation.
Process errors	Provide the student with a visual showing the actual steps needed to complete a multiplication problem (lining up the problem, multiplying, and then adding).

Activity 2: During English class, students are required to demonstrate knowledge of a subject and predicate. The assignment is to copy a model sentence from the board and divide it into two parts: subject and predicate. The first example on the board is *Mary Smith is absent from class.*

The student struggles with the assignment. Think about why this may be, and complete the following chart by listing some possible difficulties along with potential solutions. Keep in mind that the objective is to know the difference between a subject and a predicate.

Difficulty	Solution

Now compare your chart to the following chart. Did you list some of the same ideas?

Difficulty	Solution
Fine motor difficulty	Provide a copy of the assignment so the student does not have to copy from the board.
	Allow the student to draw a line between the subject and predicate or circle the subject on the paper instead of rewriting.
Understanding of concept	Present sentences orally until the student can determine the subject and predicate.
Level of reading	Provide examples at the student's reading level.

In both of the previous activities, it is important to know the objective and determine where the difficulty lies. Often the student knows the answer, but the process of getting to that answer is difficult. If a student is unable to read the words on the board, the student must copy the letters one by one, continually looking between the board and the paper. Let us illustrate this with a simple example. Copy the following sentence onto a piece of paper: *Tin kaaxtik kap-el ka'ano'ob.* Assuming that you cannot read Mayan, you need to look from the book to your paper and back to the book to copy it. It is easy to lose your place because the words have no meaning to you. Copying them takes longer, and it is easy to miss a letter or a punctuation mark because you have no clue what you are copying! Now that you have copied it, write the subject and the predicate of the sentence on your paper. This presents a problem because it is likely that even if you can read it, you do not understand it. Therefore, the reading and understanding of the language used is interfering with finding the correct answer.

Once the sentence is translated, it is easy to determine the subject and predicate. The sentence *Tin kaaxtik kap-el ka'ano'ob* is translated to "I want to buy two hammocks." Now, can you determine the subject and predicate? Of course, it is easy! For the student, the same applies. Once the obstacle is removed, the student often knows the answer. Therefore, it is very important to remember the objective (what the student must learn) and not punish the student because obstacles get in the way. Hopefully, this provides a little insight into what some students may experience when working on assignments in which the disability interferes with learning. This is an extreme example, but it was selected so that you could experience what some students experience all day long. For students who have difficulty with both reading and writing, some assignments seem like foreign language. *Ka xi'ik teech utsil!* (Good luck to you!)

In the classroom, the supervising teacher provides the guidelines and decides whether it is appropriate to help the student in this manner. Most likely, in the two previous examples, the supervising teacher would concur that when a student has demonstrated mastery (which is usually 80 percent), an appropriate use of the remaining class period would be to help the student in other academic areas.

Students with special needs often require additional support. One of the greatest difficulties with extra support is finding the time during the school day to provide the supplementary service. Frequently, students with special needs receive extra support during nonacademic periods. When this occurs repeatedly, the supplementary support becomes a punishment instead of support. So it is important, when possible, to schedule the support during the concurrent academic class periods. Optimally, when the majority of students are doing seatwork, supplementary remedial support can occur. In conjunction with the supervising teacher, determine the appropriateness of the daily assignments. Ask yourself: Is this beneficial to the student? Is it important for the student to complete the entire assignment if the student is able to demonstrate mastery when completing 50 percent of the assignment?

In many cases, daily assignments can be completed orally in a fraction of the time that it would take to complete them in a traditional manner. This may allow the extra time needed for remediation in other academic areas. Independent work periods can also be used to reinforce previously taught skills or to help the student complete required assignments. There will be times when other students in the classroom may benefit from reteaching or reinforcement of an activity. During such an activity, the classroom teacher may include other students in your group. This is legal as long as these other students do not become a permanent, consistent part of the group.

Support With Daily Assignments

This section provides ideas for adapting daily assignments. Support that is specific to certain subject areas are in other chapters of this book.

59. Modify the length of the assignment by dividing it in half and assigning only the even- or odd-numbered problems.

60. Divide the assignment into smaller segments, and have the student complete them over a period of several days.

61. Use a cover sheet with long assignments. The assignment may not feel as overwhelming to the student. The cover sheet also helps block out distracting stimuli on the page.

62. Allow the student to work with a partner or in a cooperative group. The partner or a member of the group can read the questions aloud while the student writes the answers.

63. Allow the student to respond verbally into a tape recorder.

64. If the student does not have a consumable textbook (i.e., one that can be written in), provide a photocopy of the material. Ask the student to highlight, underline, or fill in the blanks on the copy instead of copying the entire page of sentences, paragraphs, or math problems.

65. Assignment sheets will help the student organize and prioritize daily assignments. These sheets should include the due date of each assignment. (Be sure the student knows the difference between the words *do* and *due*.) Ask the student to check off the assignment when it is completed. **Form 20, Daily Assignment Log,** and **Form 21, Weekly Assignments,** can be used for this purpose. Most students use a daily assignment sheet. The weekly assignment sheet is good for projects that are divided into steps, for example, a written language assignment that includes a rough draft (due on Monday), an edited version (due on Wednesday), and a final copy (due on Friday).

66. When a student falls behind, allow the student to respond orally while you write the response. This is beneficial for the student who is continually behind due to difficulty with fine motor control. Be sure that the student continues to write some assignments on a daily basis.

67. Allow extra time for completion of assignments.

68. If conducive to the assignment, allow the student to illustrate the answer instead of responding in a written format.

69. Offer supplementary materials that coincide with the text but are at a lower reading level. Look in the teacher's guide. Textbook companies often provide extra blackline masters for different levels: beginning, intermediate, extension, extra practice, and language activities for ESL students. Some of the supplemental material may be appropriate for the student.

70. Provide parallel activities at an appropriate level. For example, if the class objective is to locate nouns in sentences on a worksheet and the student is unable to read the worksheet, try using a book at the student's level. Allow the student to write the nouns from a story. If the student is unable to read, locate objects in the classroom that are nouns.

71. General education teachers frequently provide written contracts for individual units. The contract allows for simple modification of the length of the unit by highlighting assignments that the student is responsible for completing. Most contracts include the required information and supplemental material as well. If the contract includes supplemental "fun" activities, be sure the student has the opportunity to select some of these activities. Students with disabilities spend so much time catching up that they often miss the extra activities that other students get to complete.

72. Supply the student with a pad of Post-it notes. If the student does not complete an assignment during class time, a note is placed in the student's assignment book. When the assignment is complete, the student discards the note.

73. Use the technology available in the school. Computers, word processors, and calculators will help some students complete the required work.

FOLLOWING DIRECTIONS

Every day, students must process hundreds of directions. Many students have trouble in school because they are unable to process this information. Inattention, difficulty with auditory processing, memory deficits, poor listening skills, limited receptive language, and the inability to sequence information are only a few of the reasons. No matter what the root of the problem is, it can be a very frustrating experience for the student. This section discusses strategies for both oral and written directions.

Oral Directions

74. Be sure the student is looking directly at you before you give a direction. Eye contact is important because it signifies that the student is listening.

75. Help students become aware of key words that indicate a series of directions such as *first, second, next, then,* and *finally.*

76. If the general education teacher gives directions orally, write them down and give a copy to the student to refer to as needed.

77. Do not add irrelevant information during oral directions. Keep directions concise and simple.

78. Simplify the vocabulary. Accompany verbal explanations with visual demonstrations whenever possible.

79. Divide each direction into one- or two-step components. If the directions are complex, allow the student to complete the first steps before you give additional directions.

80. Appoint a peer tutor to coach the student through multistep directions.

81. Ask the student to repeat the directions to check for understanding.

82. Use a combination of visual and auditory directions for the student. Whenever possible, consider drawing pictures of the steps.

83. Use a camera. Photograph the various steps of experiments, demonstrations, and other multistep activities. Glue the pictures to a file folder in chronological order. The student may use this folder as a visual aid. File the directions with the unit for future use.

84. For the student who continually has trouble with oral directions, practice the skills with the following activities:

Activity 1: Collect various small objects found in the classroom (e.g., pencil, pen, eraser, paper clip, staple remover, key, chalk). Place two dissimilar types of paper (e.g., lined, unlined, colored) on the student's desk. Give the student simple one- and two-step directions, and ask the student to respond. Ask the student to pay close attention because the directions will not be repeated. As the student becomes proficient, increase to multistep directions.
Sample one-step directions:

- Place your pencil in the center of the notebook paper.
- Next, put the paper clip on the red construction paper.
- Now place the key below the paper clip.
- How many objects are on your red construction paper?

Sample two-step directions:

- First, place the staple remover and the chalk in the center of the construction paper.
- Next, put the pencil at the top of the notebook paper and the pen at the bottom.
- Finally, put the key between the pen and pencil, and clip the paper clip to the top of the construction paper.

As the student becomes more proficient, increase the number of objects and the complexity of the directions.

Activity 2: For this activity, which may be adapted for any level, the student will need a piece of paper and a pencil. Once again, let the student know that it is important to pay close attention because the directions will not be repeated. Here are the sample directions:

- Write your name in the lower right corner of your paper and the date in the upper right corner.
- In the center of the paper, write a lowercase letter *a*. The lowercase letter *a* should be approximately one inch in size.

- Next, write a capital *B* in the lower left corner and a capital *C* in the upper right corner.
- Finally, draw a line to connect the three letters. When finished, fold the paper in half and put down your pencil.
- [When all students have finished, ask:] "What did you draw on the paper?" (a diagonal line)

85. Make audio recordings of daily assignments, and include the due dates. This will allow the student to listen to the directions as many times as needed. Encourage the student to list incomplete assignments in the homework notebook.

86. If the student has a hearing impairment, appoint a peer to cue the student when directions are given orally or over the intercom system. Always check for understanding.

Written Directions

87. Provide directions in sequential order. If there are multiple steps, number the steps or place a colored dot between each step.

88. Allow extra time for the student to copy the directions for assignments. If the student is unable to copy from a distant model, ask a peer to write or dictate the directions to the student.

89. Ask the student to read written directions at least twice before asking for assistance. Allow extra time for underlining or highlighting key words and phrases.

90. Always check for understanding before the student begins the assignment.

91. For the visually impaired student, always give test directions, assignments, and other important instructions orally.

92. Place a piece of yellow acetate over the printed page to enhance the contrast for students with a visual impairment.

93. Use black felt-tip pens to trace over or darken large print for students with low vision.

LARGE-GROUP INSTRUCTION

A portion of a student's day is spent listening to material presented orally. This may be in the form of a class lecture, a video, a movie, a speaker, or learning from peers. Classroom lectures are often difficult for students with special needs, especially for those who have difficulty with auditory processing.

94. While listening to the lecture, write the goals and objectives of the lesson for the student. Discuss the goals and objectives before beginning the follow-up assignments.

95. Review previous lessons, notes, and vocabulary words. Link new facts and materials to previously learned information.

96. When reviewing material, present only the relevant information. Use nouns when possible. Leave out pronouns such as *it, him, her, them,* and *those.* The continual use of pronouns causes confusion, especially if the student did not grasp the subject of the lecture.

97. Simplify the vocabulary when reviewing lecture notes with the student.

98. When presenting material orally, frequently ask the student to summarize the new information learned. Ask direct questions to check for understanding.

99. Be sure the student removes all unnecessary materials from the desktop before the lecture begins. If the student is required to take notes during a presentation, two sharpened pencils, paper, and a highlighter should be the only objects on top of the desk.

NOTE-TAKING SKILLS

Taking notes during class can be a difficult process. Think about the last time you attended a class or workshop. Did you take notes on the syllabus provided? Perhaps you recorded the information to listen to in the car on the way home. Did you jot down key words and phrases? Or did you write entire phrases verbatim? Perhaps you were able to generalize the information and fill in a chart or a graph. When the presenter stated, "This is important!" did you furiously try to write every word? As adults, we use many strategies at different times and for different situations. Note taking is not a simple skill. It requires the student to process information both auditorily and visually. The student must then output the information in a written format. Students must be taught strategies to take notes successfully.

100. Before the presentation, read the discussion questions (if available) to the student. This will help the student focus on the most important information.

101. Teach key phrases such as *please remember this, this point is very important,* or *write this down*. General education teachers use these words frequently when making key points.

102. Encourage the student to take notes in his or her own words.

103. Teach common abbreviations for note taking (see **Form 22, Common Abbreviations for Note Taking**). Students can add their own abbreviations to the list.

104. Provide the student with an outline of the main topics before a new lesson is presented. Provide ample space so that the student may take notes directly on the outline sheet. **Form 23, Chapter Outline,** may be used.

105. This strategy works well if a student has time immediately following the lecture to go over the notes. Fold a piece of notebook paper in half vertically to form two columns. Label the left column "Topic" and the right column "Details." During the lecture, the student writes the topic and words to support the details. Immediately after the lecture, the student completes the detail column by expanding on the key words written.

106. If students are required to compare and contrast information, provide the student with a chart. **Form 24, Compare and Contrast,** has a column to list attributes along with space to compare two objects. Venn diagrams may also be used to compare and contrast.

107. Timelines help document chronological information. Provide a timeline to the student in advance, and demonstrate its use. If you know the specific events and dates in advance, insert several to help the student get started. The student fills in the remaining information. If the student is able to complete all the steps alone, allow him or her to do so.

108. Teach the student to write only key words when there is not enough time to complete the entire thought. Select some of the most common abbreviations from Form 22. You can assist the student with the organization later.

109. If the student is unable to take notes, allow a peer to take notes for the student or photocopy the classroom teacher's notes. Part of your job description may be to take notes for the student. If notes are provided to the student, it is important that he or she continue to practice the skill. For visually impaired students, it may be more important to listen or to use a computer to type in notes.

110. Demonstrate how to highlight the important information in the notes after the lecture.

111. If the general education teacher uses an overhead projector with transparencies, the student with low vision should look directly into the overhead projector while the transparency is projected onto the wall. Many classrooms now use interactive whiteboards, such as SMART Boards, which allow material to be enlarged or notes printed off. The vision teacher can discuss options with you.

112. An overhead projector, whiteboard, or SMART Board assists students with a hearing impairment. It allows the student to simultaneously see the presentation and read the teacher's lips. Make sure the student is seated in an appropriate location.

113. Make an audio or video recording of the presentation. Allow the student to take it home for review.

ORGANIZATIONAL SKILLS

Organizational skills frequently need to be taught to both general and special education students. Simple skills such as keeping pencils and crayons in the proper place, hanging coats on the coat hook, keeping personal space organized, and returning items to the proper location should begin being emphasized as soon as students enter school. Assignment sheets and homework books should be incorporated as soon as students begin to have homework assignments. As students reach middle school, organization becomes more complex. They often have five to seven class periods, and different materials are needed for each class. Frequently, disorganized students complete assignments but misplace them; as a result, assignments are turned in late or not at all. As a paraprofessional, a significant amount of your time is spent helping students organize. Some students also need help with organization of time and physical space.

I highly recommend the book *Winning the Study Game: Learning How to Succeed in School* (Greene, 2002) for students with learning disabilities, those who are considered at risk, and Title I students in Grades 6–11 who need a comprehensive study skills program. The readability level of approximately 5.5 allows students to focus on acquiring the skills needed without having to struggle with reading the material. The skills may be taught in isolation or sequentially as a comprehensive program.

Organizing the Environment

At the beginning of the school year, some students benefit from having a simplified map of the school. Highlight the student's classroom areas, and include arrows to indicate the most direct route between classes.

114. Some students need to know in advance what is going to occur. If a daily schedule is not posted, create one. This helps students anticipate what is about to occur. Some students are very dependent on routine, and a small change can upset them for hours. For these students, discuss schedule changes early in the day.

115. The majority of classrooms have a specific location to hand in daily assignments and homework. Encourage the student to turn in material upon arriving to class. If the location changes frequently, find a peer to help the student.

116. Provide the student with a gentle reminder several minutes before the class period ends. The reminder may be visual, such as pointing to the clock, or oral. Often, disorganized students need several extra minutes to organize their materials before a transition.

117. Some students require special seating. The student with a hearing impairment must have a special location in the classroom. If the classroom has tables in lieu of desks, the student should be seated in a location that allows him or her to see the board and the teacher without having to turn around. The student should not have his or her back to the teacher. If the seating is not conducive to the student's learning, speak with the supervising teacher.

118. For the student who is easily distracted, special seating may also be needed. The student should be seated away from windows, doors, the pencil sharpener, and high-traffic areas.

Student Organization

The majority of students would like to be organized. They just do not always know how. For some students, their bedroom or study area is disorganized, resulting in misplaced assignments. Encourage students to use the same strategies learned at school in the home environment also.

119. Do not make assumptions about students' organizational knowledge. If the classroom teacher expects students to organize material in a specific manner, keep a model notebook that students can reference when organizing their own material.

120. Color-code pocket folders for each subject area. If possible, coordinate the folders with the colors of the textbooks. If the math textbook is predominantly red, the pocket folder should be red also. Insert a pencil, a pen, paper, and other necessary items in the pocket folder. Each pocket folder can have its own set of supplies.

121. If individual pocket folders are confusing and the material is still getting misplaced, encourage the student to use a three-ring binder. All of the student's folders and papers as well as the assignment book may be inserted into the binder. With this method, the assignment remains in the binder until it is time to turn it in. All important papers can be three-hole-punched and inserted. At the upper grade levels, the student will need several binders to accommodate all subject areas. The majority of students go to their lockers during lunch, so it is wise to have one binder for the morning and another for the afternoon.

Greene (2002) recommends doing the following:

- Buy or make subject dividers to include in the binder.
- Section 1 of the binder should include the assignment sheet. (You may reproduce Form 20 or 21.)

- Section 1 should also include a personal study schedule. *Winning the Study Game* (Greene, 2002) provides a method for estimating the amount of study time needed for each subject area. This enables students to create their own weekly study schedules. **Form 25, Weekly Study Schedule,** is a modified version of a home study schedule. Students may use this form to develop their own personal study schedules. The student blocks the times that cannot be changed, such as extracurricular activities, music lessons, and church activities. The student then inserts a daily study time. Free-time activities are inserted last. Every student should have study time and free time daily. If these do not fit into the schedule, the student needs to cut back on some extracurricular activities. The student should practice using the schedule and add additional study time if needed.
- Section 2 should include individual tabs for each subject area; this is where all papers may be saved and stored.
- Store all important papers in the binder. Greene (2002) suggests inserting a three-hole-punched manila envelope into the binder for this purpose.

122. Tape a large manila envelope to the inside of the student's desk. If assignments are not complete, the student can slip the paper into the envelope to complete later.

123. For older students, provide manila envelopes to help keep materials for large projects or assignments with multiple components together in one place.

124. Help the student clean and organize the desk or locker at least once a week. Organize the papers into three piles: file into folders, take home, or toss.

125. Be specific when helping a student organize. Be sure that every handout is clearly labeled. Each should have a title and a clear indicator of the binder section to which it belongs. With written assignments, it is easy to confuse a social studies rough draft with an English rough draft. Proper headings help the student organize paper into the appropriate folders or sections of the binder.

126. Ask students to share their organizational tips. Keep a list of ideas so you can help future students figure out the system that works best for them.

127. Encourage the student to use a homework book or an assignment sheet. Help the student learn how to prioritize assignments. Some students need a weekly or monthly calendar to understand the concept of time. **Form 26, Priority Assignment Sheet,** may be used to rank assignments and calculate the approximate time needed to complete each assignment.

128. List assignments along with the approximate amount of time it will take to complete them. Divide large projects such as research papers into smaller blocks. Some students have no concept of time. Without providing guidelines and time frames, they frequently leave an assignment until the last minute. Students frequently need help prioritizing assignments and managing time.

129. Supply each student with a "Things to Do Today" list (see **Form 27, My To-Do List)**. Ask the student to write on the list what needs to be done. The student can include specific reminders.

130. Ask a peer to help monitor assignments. The peer may help the student place the assignments into the correct folders.

131. Allow students who have difficulty remembering to do homework assignments to call home and leave a message. Be sure the message includes the subject and the page numbers of the assignment. A simple verbal cue such as "Do math" usually is not enough.

132. Check out an extra set of textbooks for home use. Many times a student will list assignments in the assignment book but will forget to bring home the textbooks.

133. Create a simple daily checklist, and tape it on top of the student's desk or in a notebook. The student may write the assignments with the due dates and cross off each assignment when complete. Whatever doesn't get crossed off becomes homework.

134. When an assignment is complete, encourage the student to turn it in immediately. It is frustrating when a student must redo an assignment because it got lost. Special arrangements may need to be made with the classroom teacher to allow the student to turn in an assignment early. If this is not an option, keep a special folder for the student to insert papers until they can be turned in.

135. Plastic bags work well to store extra pencils, crayons, markers, and supplies. At the elementary level, the student can keep several individual bags of supplies. When transitioning to another class, the student will not have to search for supplies.

136. Spot-check students at the beginning and the end of transition times. Many students miss directions because they are organizing their supplies.

137. If assisting the student with check-in and check-out times, go to the student's classroom so that the he or she will not miss valuable class time or important directions. **Form 28, Checklist: Materials to Take Home,** may be reproduced for this purpose.

138. Teach the student to use self-talk methods. Ask the student to verbalize the steps after the teacher has given multistep directions.

NOTES

10

Reading

Children are likely to live up to what you believe of them.

Charlotte "Lady Bird" Johnson

Many students who receive special education services encounter difficulty in the area of reading. Chapter 8 includes strategies to help students with reading, specifically textbook accommodations, creating alternate forms of material such as audiotapes, and previewing material. This chapter deals specifically with helping students learn to read by using certain strategies for decoding, comprehension, and vocabulary.

STRATEGIES FOR STRUGGLING READERS

For the student who is unable to read or struggles with reading, the school day presents a unique challenge. The most common type of struggling reader is a student with a learning disability. More than likely, this student has average to above-average intelligence and understands the concepts taught, but struggles with the reading level. This is very common at the secondary level as reading becomes more difficult, resulting in a larger discrepancy between the struggling student's reading and that of his or her peer group.

Technology

As technology advances, new software becomes less expensive and more readily available for student use. This is without doubt positive news for students with special needs. As the demands of the curriculum increase, the reading levels and expectations for students also increase. In the primary grades, educators remediate and provide reading instruction. However, as students advance to high school and continue to struggle, technology is a viable option. A number of the following programs have multiple uses for all curriculum areas. Some allow for textbook editing, and many include written language components as well. Many options are available, though, and this list is not an endorsement of a particular product. It is simply intended to provide an overview of some frequently used programs:

- *Cicero Text Reader:* This program uses the computer and scanner to create a reading machine for students. Printed text is scanned and translated into speech, Braille, or a text document that can be adjusted, edited, and saved.
- *ClaroRead PLUS:* This helps struggling readers and writers create, read, view, and check text. It features powerful reading and writing assistance toolbars, text-to-speech capabilities, and easy-to use features.
- *Kurzweil 3000:* This program combines scanning and reading applications that allow easier conversion from printed text to audio feedback. It also helps students by highlighting the line of print and individual words as they are read.
- *Ovation Reading Machine:* This is an easy-to-use solution for reading that can scan and convert to audio a wide variety of printed material, including books, mail, newspapers, and magazines.
- *Scan N Talk Ultra:* This set, which includes both the software and a scanner, gives students increased access to the printed word.
- *Writing with Symbols 2000:* This word- and picture-processing software gives users the option to have a picture or symbol appear with each word.

139. Search for alternative resources for the student. You can often find books that have an easier readability level, simplified vocabulary, larger print, and an abundance of pictures. In areas such as science and social studies, libraries usually have numerous titles. Look for similar content presented in other media formats such as videos and DVDs.

140. Rewrite the text on the computer using simplified vocabulary. Highlight only the information that the student is required to learn.

141. If a student is involved with online research, use the AutoSummarize function in, for example, Microsoft Word. With AutoSummarize, the computer summarizes the selected text from sources such as Internet downloads or scanned text. Key phrases can be highlighted. Although not completely accurate, it is a useful tool for students who are overwhelmed by a large volume of print.

READING DECODING

Reading is a complex skill. It is a systematic process, and each new skill builds on a previously learned skill. The first step is to be able to decode written symbols, and to do this students must visually remember random shapes and connect these shapes to a sound (sound–symbol relationship). Of course, the sounds are often inconsistent, and there are subtle differences between them (e.g., the sounds associated with *c* and *g*), which cause further confusion. Once the sounds are learned, they are combined to make words. Of course, some words are phonetic, whereas others, frequently referred to as *sight words*, cannot be sounded out and must be memorized. Add blends, diphthongs, suffixes, prefixes, and irregular words to the mix, and it is a wonder that students learn to read at all! Students often have gaps in one or many of the previous areas that hinder the process of learning to read. In addition to providing support for students with daily activities, you may also help them with reinforcement activities. This section provides strategies for working with students at the very basic level of decoding.

142. Some students have difficulty discriminating between subtle sounds. Some may have difficulty in the area of auditory processing; others may have trouble due to intermittent hearing loss, which is frequently overlooked. If you believe that the student is not hearing the sounds correctly, tell the supervising teacher.

143. Check to be sure that the student knows the sounds associated with the letters. If the student does know them, review the sounds by selecting, and varying your use of, some of the following activities:

Alphabet activities. Form 29, Alphabet Activities, provides two activities for each letter of the alphabet. Although developed for Chapter 11, Written Language, many of the activities are adaptable for sound recognition.

Letter books. These little books can be created in any manner and include a variety of material. The only criterion is that the activity must relate to the letter. For example, an M book may include pictures the student has drawn (or cut out from magazines) that begin with the *mmm* sound. The student may create silly sentences to illustrate, such as *Messy Mary makes mud pies in March!* The M book may include a collection of mazes. This is a simple way to reinforce letters and sounds.

Word chains. This simple activity takes only a few minutes. To create word chains beginning with the *mmm* sound, the first person begins with an *m* word. The second person must remember the previous word and add another to the chain. For example, the first student says, "Monday starts with the *mmm* sound." The next student repeats and adds a word: "Monday and monkey start with *mmm*." The next student repeats and adds another word: Monday, monkey, and moon start with *mmm*." This not only helps with letter–sound association, but also facilitates word retrieval and memory building.

Drill and practice. This simple activity takes only a few minutes daily. Write the letters of the alphabet on index cards, or reproduce **Form 30, Alphabet Cards.** Randomly select five cards. Flash the cards, one at a time, and ask students to say the sound of each card. If the student responds correctly, make a tally mark on the back of the card. When the student correctly responds three times, the card is placed into a Sounds I Know pile, and a new card is added to the practice pile. The student should always have five cards in the practice pile. If the student answers incorrectly, the card remains in the Sounds to Practice pile. Once a week, review the sounds from the Sounds I Know pile. If the student misses a sound at the end of the week, it is placed back into the Sounds to Practice pile. This activity is appropriate to use for sight words, vocabulary words, math facts, and more. **Tip:** Recipe boxes are great for organizing the cards.

Riddles. Younger children enjoy making riddles. Vary the riddles depending on the grade level. For example, for a younger student you may simply say, "I am thinking of something that starts with M. It is located in the sky at night. Can you guess?" (answer: moon). For an older student you may make it a little more difficult by going from general to specific. For example: "I am thinking of an object that begins with M." (Student guesses *magnet*.) "I am thinking of a round, bright object." (Student guesses *lightbulb*.) "I am thinking of a round, bright object located in the sky." (Student guesses *sun*.) "I am thinking of a round, bright object located in the sky at night." (Student guesses *moon*.) Ask the student to create his or her own riddles.

144. If the student has mastered the letter sounds, it is time to introduce blending. Word patterns are grouped into word families. The supervising teacher provides the order to reinforce the word families. The following activities will help you get started:

Flip charts. Write each consonant on a separate index card (or select alphabet cards from Form 30). Practice adding different initial consonants to the word family to make the words *man, can, fan, tan,* and so on. Continue until the student is proficient. For independent practice, use a hole-punch to cut a hole into the top center of each card, and place the cards onto a metal ring. Give the student an index card with the word family *an*. The student flips the consonant cards to practice reading the new words. **Form 31, Common Word Families,** lists the beginning and advanced word families. Older students can use this sheet to practice reading and creating new words.

Magnetic letters or magnetic letter cards. Provide the student with magnetic letters, and encourage the student to put the sounds together to make words. Color-code the vowels, and explain to students that often with three-letter words the vowel is in the middle.

Memory match. Students also enjoy memory games. Find pictures of pairs of rhyming words from magazines, and glue them to index cards. Some easily found pairs include *hat-cat, car-star,* and *man-can.* Start with three pairs, and increase the number as the student becomes more efficient. Also, include the written word so that the student can visually see the word family.

Nonsense stories. Create small, simple books with nonsense sentences for students to illustrate. For example, *Jan sat on a tan pan, The tan Jan had a fan.*

Rhyming words. Rhyming is a natural way to teach word families. Develop oral rhyming patterns with students by using a riddle format, such as "I am thinking of something you wear on your head that rhymes with cat" (answer: hat). Dr. Seuss books are fun to read and are full of silly nonsense rhymes.

145. Many Web sites provide a systematic approach to phonics. The games and activities on *Starfall* (www.starfall.com) are varied and fun for young students, and the site includes printable activity sheets. This great site provides a wide selection of activities for all beginning stages of reading.

146. Provide students with their own set of phonics posters and flash cards. Two sites that have free appropriate material are *MES-English* (www.mes-english.com) and *Adrian Bruce's Educational Teaching Resources* (www.adrianbruce.com). Take time to explore additional free material that may be appropriate for reinforcement activities on these sites.

147. **Form 32, Basic Phonics Rules,** is a simple list of the most common rules for your reference. Students may use this form as a handy reference sheet.

148. Students need to learn Dolch Words and Fry Instant Words (see #149). Why are students expected to learn these words? First, many are sight words; therefore, a student who tries to decode the word will likely be unsuccessful. Second, these are high-frequency words, which means that they are used repeatedly. In fact, the hundred most common words actually make up about 50 percent of all the material a student

reads. If a student is able to read these words automatically, he or she will be a more successful reader. **Form 33, Dolch Word List,** includes the 220 most frequently found words in children's books. These words are usually learned in early elementary school, although some students may need reinforcement for many years. These words provide a good base for beginning reading. There is also a Dolch scale to determine a child's approximate reading level:

0–75 words: Preprimer level
76–120 words: Primer level
121–170 words: First grade
171–210 words: Second grade
Above 210: Third grade

Search online for Dolch Sight Words, and you will find hundreds of printable activities to reinforce these words.

149. The Fry Instant Word List contains the 600 most common words in the English language. The first 100 words make up almost 50 percent of written language. By learning these hundred words, a student is on the way to becoming a successful reader. **Form 34, Instant Words**, lists the hundred most commonly used words in the English language. Search for Fry Instant Words online to find the remaining 500 words and activities for reinforcement.

150. Sight word recognition helps students become more fluent in reading. The following is a drill to reinforce sight words:

Provide the student with a set of sight-word cards. To begin, give the student six cards (two copies of each sight word).
Step 1: Show the student a sample card, and ask the student to find the words that match the model. Continue until the student consistently matches the word.
Step 2: Show the student the sample for several seconds. Remove the sample. Ask the student to find the matching cards.
Step 3: Ask the student to select specific cards without a model.
Step 4: Shuffle the cards. Show the student one card at a time, and ask the student to read the card.

151. For Sight Word Bingo, create a five-by-five grid or copy **Form 35, Bingo Game Grid**. Randomly write 25 sight words onto the grid. (For some students a three-by-three grid may be appropriate, and **Form 36, Tic-Tac-Toe Grid,** may be substituted.) Randomly select a word from the sight word pile, and ask the student to find the word on the grid. The game terminates when the student gets five in a row. The Bingo grid can be used to review sounds, vocabulary words, math facts, spelling, and more.

152. Create a three-by-three Tic-Tac-Toe grid (or copy Form 36). Randomly select nine sight words. The student must read the sight word before placing the X or O onto the grid. The game proceeds as regular Tic-Tac-Toe. The nine-square grid can be adapted for many different reinforcement activities.

153. Additional material to reinforce sight words can be found at *Teacher2Teacher* (www.createdbyteachers.com). This Web site has free material (click on the Free Stuff icon), which you can use to reinforce many areas of reading. The site also includes phrase lists, noun lists, and checklists to record mastery.

READING COMPREHENSION

Some students struggle so much with the reading that it is difficult for them to understand the context of the material. Some students may read word by word, trying to sound out each one. Others may put effort into sounding part of it and then simply guess at the remaining part, at times inserting words that make no sense at all. On the other hand, you may encounter students who read flawlessly but have difficulty with language processing and do not understand what they have read. In addition to providing textbook accommodations for these students, you can implement the following additional strategies and material to help students with these difficulties.

154. Check the level of reading difficulty. Ask the student to read several paragraphs and paraphrase them. Determine whether the reading material is at the independent, instructional, or frustration level:

Independent level: The student reads the material easily and provides the correct answers to the questions asked.

Instructional level: The student is able to read the material but stumbles over some of the words. The student is able to provide correct answers to the follow-up questions.

Frustration level: The student struggles with the reading, and there are many unknown words. The student is unable to answer the follow-up questions.

155. Determining the reading level also helps you determine the required level of support. For example, if the curriculum material is at the frustration level, the student will need a great deal of support. If the reading is at the independent level, the student may be able to complete the work independently. When helping students select personal reading material, steer them toward material that is at their independent level.

156. Summarization is an important tool to help the student remember what he or she has read. When reading aloud or if the student is reading alone, ask the student to stop reading after each section and write a few sentences about what was read. This helps with retention.

157. Ask the student to develop comprehension questions while reading. The questions can be asked to others in the group. This activity helps students think about what they have read.

158. Some students stumble over words when reading aloud, but still are able to answer questions related the material. Some students retain more when reading silently. If the student prefers to read silently periodically, ask the student to provide a quick oral summary of the material. If the student is able to do this accurately, he or she can continue to read alone.

159. When the student reads aloud, use **Form 37, Word List,** to keep a list of the commonly misread words to reinforce later. Also, make note of the incorrect words that the student inserted. Look for decoding patterns that may need correction.

160. If material is difficult for the student to read, reduce the amount of reading, divide it into segments, or use a shared reading procedure that allows the student to alternate between reading and listening.

161. Keep a list of the items the student must learn. Spend additional time on these areas and provide continual reinforcement.

162. Provide the student with a chapter outline so that the student can learn to list topics and supporting details. Form 23 is a basic outline that provides a space to list the main idea and four supporting detail sentences. As the student begins to outline, complete the outline together or provide the topic sentence and ask the student to look for the supporting details. As the student becomes more proficient, he or she will be able to do it alone.

163. Develop background knowledge. The more that new knowledge is based on previously learned knowledge, the more the student will retain. If the student is reading about Australia, ask the student to tell you what he or she already knows and try to incorporate this information into the new unit of study.

164. Visualization is another technique that aids with comprehension. Ask the students to close his or her eyes while you read a short descriptive passage. Let's assume the passage is related to the circus. Ask the student, "What do you see and hear? What do you smell? What does the circus tent look like? What animals do you see? What are the people doing?" Practice this strategy frequently and encourage the student to use it on his or her own. Visualization helps with retention.

165. Organizers help students see relationships and therefore help increase comprehension. Specific organizers help students keep track of details, organize chronological events, distinguish fact from opinion, or compare and contrast people. Organizers are easy to create, and they are an important tool to help students retain what they have learned.

Form 38, Story Organizer, helps the student organize a story. By listing the main characters and important events and summarizing the story, the student retains more information. Form 38 includes several blank sections to list additional material that the student should recall. This form can also be used to help the student organize thoughts when writing a story.

Form 24 helps the student compare two places, people, or events. The student lists the attribute in the first column and the comparisons in the next two columns. The following sample would be the result of the student comparing Colorado and Florida:

Form 24: Sample Compare and Contrast

Attribute	Colorado	Florida
Population	4,500,000+	17,000,000+
Major industries	Tourism, food products, printing and publishing	Oranges, tourism, electrical equipment

Timelines are another useful tool because the student can easily create them to chart and document events that happen in chronological order.

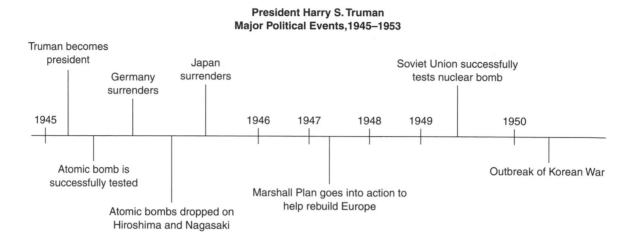

166. Create resource packets to help the student with projects and research assignments. The packets may contain project outlines, reference articles (which can be read together and whose important information can be highlighted), key vocabulary, visual aids, step-by-step guidelines, and any additional material that will help the student complete the project successfully.

VOCABULARY DEVELOPMENT

Vocabulary is an important part of learning. A strong vocabulary helps students understand the curriculum better and read more fluently. There are two types of vocabulary: oral and print. Oral vocabulary refers to words that are used in speaking and that are recognized when listening. Print vocabulary refers to the words that are recognized when reading.

167. For some students, reading words is easy but understanding them is not. **Form 39, Common Prefixes and Suffixes,** is an appropriate handout for the upper-level student. By dividing the word into syllables and examining the components, the student often is able to make an educated guess at the meaning. Analyzing the word helps the student determine the meaning.

168. Practice dividing words into syllables by finding the base words. If the student is unable to find the base word, it will be difficult to look it up in the dictionary or thesaurus.

169. Form 39 can also be used to expand the student's vocabulary. Provide the student with the base word, and ask the student to add suffixes and prefixes to make new words.

Base Word	Add Prefix	Add Suffix
form	reform	reformed, reforming
form	inform	informed, informing, information
form	deform	deformed, deforms
form		forming
form		formation

170. When a student encounters a new vocabulary word, provide strategies to decipher the meaning. Obviously, these steps cannot be followed with every unknown word, but they provide the student with a strategy to determine word meanings when reading silently.

Ask the student the following questions: "Have you seen this word before? Does the previous sentence provide a clue to what the word may mean?" Ask the student to read the sentence, omitting the word: "Can you insert a word starting with the beginning sound that makes sense?" Break the word into syllables: "Does the word have a base word that you know?" If the student still is unable to figure out the word, have the student look up the base word in the dictionary.

171. A thesaurus is a wonderful tool for vocabulary development. Note specific words that the student uses in daily conversations. Select a word, and ask the student to select a synonym from a thesaurus to use in place of the word. Practice using the word. Have the student keep track of how many times he or she is able to use the word throughout the school day.

172. Practice charting unknown words. **Form 40, Charting New Vocabulary,** can be used as a template.

Vocabulary Word: *persuade*	
What does the word mean?	**What is an antonym for this word?**
To get someone to do something; to convince someone	dissuade
Use the word in a sentence.	**Use the antonym in a sentence.**
I persuaded my mom to let me drive the car to the concert.	My father dissuaded her and offered to drive.
List additional synonyms for this word. influence, convince, win over, sway	

173. Create a Word of the Day list to expand the student's vocabulary. Discuss the meaning and use the word throughout the day. (If you would like to expand your vocabulary, you can select a word, too!) As vocabulary increases, comprehension will also increase. Some Web sites that offer a word of the day include *Merriam-Webster's Word Central* (www.wordcentral.com) and *SuperKids* (www.superkids.com).

174. Reinforce and discuss academic vocabulary from the textbooks prior to use. This helps the student better understand the upcoming academic material and units. The supervising teacher provides the list, or you can scan upcoming units for boldfaced words.

175. Develop vocabulary review pages to use with students. Define each vocabulary word in accordance with the context of the story or unit, and then list any additional meanings that the word may have. Because many words have multiple meanings, when previewing vocabulary with students, use the definition first that corresponds to the lesson.

176. Discuss the degree of words with students. Explain that many words have synonyms that range from cool to hot. For example, the overused word *said* includes various degrees. It can mean whispered, murmured, moaned, exclaimed, yelled, or screamed depending on the usage.

177. Ask the student to create charts of synonyms for commonly used words. Have the students create synonym word webs to keep as a reference.

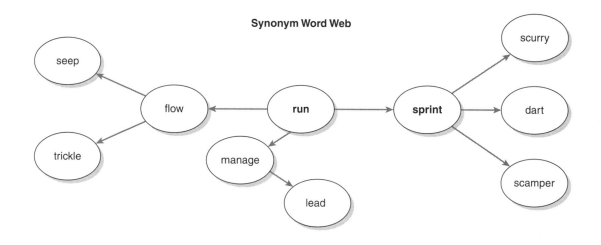

Synonym Word Web

178. Look for activities to enhance vocabulary. Web sites that offer such activities include *Vocabulary.com* (www.vocabulary.com), *edHelper* (www.edhelper.com), and others mentioned earlier in this chapter.

STUDENTS WITH VISUAL DIFFICULTIES

Many students have vision that is correctable with glasses. These students (unless they have a disability) are not served in special education. Some, however, have low vision and need support in the classroom. Students with low vision have heightened auditory and tactile senses, so loud noises may startle them and small things such as clothing tags may irritate them. These students frequently have a heightened awareness of the environment, which helps compensate for the low vision. If it appears as though they are not listening, often they are relying on their auditory skills or perhaps giving their eyes a rest. If you see these students wandering around the class, it may not be intentional; it may be that they simply cannot locate the group. For students with low vision, consistency is important in all aspects of the day.

179. The student with visual difficulties often tires easily when reading and may need frequent breaks.

180. Make sure the lighting in the work area is good.

181. Do not require the student to share reading material because the student may need to hold the material at a specific angle to be able to read it.

182. The student may need an index card or a ruler to track sentences and keep his or her place in the book.

183. Allow preferential seating for board work activity or if the student requests it. The student may need a photocopy to have a close-up model.

184. Avoid giving the student cluttered paper. Allow ample space between lines and sections of text. White space is good.

185. Keep the student's books and materials in the same place. The student may be able to see large features throughout the room, but details are often difficult.

186. Do not assume that because the student wears glasses that the student sees the same as everyone else in the class. For some students, glasses improve the vision but the vision is still impaired. Glasses do not help all students with low vision.

187. Do not ask the student if he or she can see. A student with low vision sees differently than those with 20/20 vision. If asked, the student will often say that he or she sees well, but the student's definition of *well* and yours may not be the same.

188. If you work with a student with a visual impairment, be sure you understand the print size, lighting level, supplemental aids, and accommodations available to the student. If in doubt, contact the vision teacher.

NOTES

11

Written Language

Thought is the blossom; language the bud; action is the fruit behind it.

Ralph Waldo Emerson

Understanding written language is a complex process. Students may encounter difficulty with written language for many different reasons. Some may have trouble formulating and organizing their ideas on paper; while other students in the classroom are busy filling their paper with ideas, these students may simply stare at the paper, unsure of how to sequence the ideas or organize their thoughts. Some students encounter difficulty with the grammar and syntax of written language, whereas others have expressive language limitations and are unable to find the words needed to express themselves. Reluctant writers may not want to write because, more often than not, their papers are returned covered with corrections; they may be discouraged and feel that it is not worth the time or the effort. A small number of students experience difficulty with fine motor control and may be unable to write within the lines of the standard-size classroom paper; these students may be allowed to use the computer for some activities but still should be required to complete paper-and-pencil tasks daily to develop the skill. Due to one or several of the previous limitations, you will encounter reluctant writers. It is important to encourage all of their attempts, no matter how small, and place the emphasis on the students' ideas instead of on sentence structure and spelling.

One question that frequently arises is whether students should be able to print or be required to write in cursive. With cursive writing, some of the spatial difficulties related to writing are eliminated because the letters are continuous and connected to one another. Letter reversal may also be eliminated with cursive writing. Once students becomes fluent with cursive writing, it is often faster and easier for them to write. Some students may be allowed to print, others may be required to learn cursive writing, and some may use a combination of both. The special education team determines the appropriate method.

PREWRITING STAGE

A large discrepancy exists between some students' writing and that of their peers. Some students may be in a prewriting stage. If this is the case, parallel or supplemental activities can be provided according to their individualized education plan. The following section on fine motor development provides activities to help students increase fine motor control. Until students have this control, they will not be able to form letters. Many of these activities can also be used to reinforce prereading skills.

Fine Motor Development

The following activities involve the use of manipulative objects to help build the strength and dexterity a student will need in order to hold a pencil correctly:

189. With palms facing together and fingers slightly curved, roll the play dough (or any other similar material) into balls.

190. Roll play dough into tiny peas using the fingertips and use a toothpick to pick up the tiny peas.

191. Use toothpicks, pegs, and cookie cutters to make designs in the play dough.

192. Cut the play dough into strips using a plastic knife.

193. Use a large tweezers to pick up tiny objects such as Cheerios.

194. Tear paper into strips, and crumple the paper into balls using one hand only.

195. Peel stickers off the master sheet, and create designs and pictures on paper.

196. Use silly putty to copy designs from comic books.

197. Play board games. Picking up cards from a deck, moving small objects around a game board, and shaking and retrieving dice all require fine motor skills.

198. Practice self-help skills such as lacing shoes, zipping coats, and buttoning clothes.

Letter Formation

199. Practice letter formation with the use of any of the following materials. The emphasis for this activity may be placed on sound–symbol association because many of the practice activities can be used with letters. It is important to vary the activities to maintain a high level of interest.

Pudding: Prepare the pudding, and pour it into a cake pan. The student writes letters in the pudding and can then clean his or her fingers by licking them. Practice both capital (upper case) and lowercase letters. Check with the supervising teacher to determine whether to use the term *capital* or *uppercase* so that the student learns the same terminology in all settings.

Commercially colored sand, chalk, or salt: Although not as much fun as pudding, these materials work equally well for the student to use in forming letters.

Finger paints: Students love finger painting, but this is rarely the chosen method because it is quite messy. With finger paints, the student spreads the paint on a piece of glossy paper and then proceeds to write the letters in the paint, saying the letter name while doing so. This may be done on a desktop or an easel.

Pipe cleaners: The student bends a pipe cleaner into letter shapes. The student may trace around the pipe cleaner once the letter is formed.

Play dough or clay: While saying the letter aloud, the student molds the letter with clay or play dough.

Magnetic letters: Provide the student with a set of capital and lowercase letters. Ask the student to match the lowercase letter to the corresponding capital letter.

200. Ask the student to trace large objects from a coloring book using tracing paper.

201. If the student is unable to trace, draw the outline with a pencil and have the student trace your example with crayon. Once the student becomes proficient with tracing bold outlines, change the original design to short lines and, finally, to small dots. Another option is to enlarge pictures or cartoons with an overhead projector and allow the student to trace and color the pictures.

202. Ask the student to reproduce simple shapes from a model. Use simple pictures from art instruction books, learn-to-draw books, or preschool coloring books.

203. Make alphabet puzzles. Create an 8½" x 11" letter template on tag board. Make two copies of the letter. Keep one as a model, and cut the other into two to four pieces depending on the student's ability level. The student can place the pieces on the model to recreate the letter or put the puzzle together without the template. Store the puzzle pieces in individual envelopes.

204. Allow the student to work with dot-to-dot pictures. Use A, B, C pictures for prereading practice and 1, 2, 3 pictures for math.

205. Special activities may be created for additional practice for each letter of the alphabet. Some activities are listed on Form 29.

206. Allow the student to illustrate his or her response instead of writing it.

207. Ask the special education teacher if letter templates are available. Tracing these templates helps the student develop fine motor control.

208. Inquire whether commercially made paper with raised lines is available. This paper works well in practicing letter formation because the raised lines help guide the student.

209. Allow the student to dictate a story to you or a peer. Later, the student can practice reading the story and tracing the letters.

210. Provide the student with material to copy from a close-up model. As the student becomes more proficient, he or she may copy from the board or the overhead. The outcome for the student may be a handwriting goal.

211. Incorporate other fine motor developmental activities such as stringing beads, making pegboard designs, using sewing cards, weaving, cutting, or using clay during the written language blocks.

ONE WORD AT A TIME

Once a student has developed some proficiency with fine motor control, it is time to begin initial written language activities. The following ideas are for students who are working with individual words and progressing to four to five words joined. Some students may need to copy the words from a model, whereas others may be able to write the words on their own.

212. The student may begin to label items with one word. These are some ideas that can be incorporated with labeling:

- The student cuts out and pastes random pictures onto a large piece of construction paper. The student dictates the word for the label and then copies it onto the paper from a model.
- The student selects a category (e.g., food, animals, toys). The student looks for pictures, pastes them onto construction paper or creates a small book, and then labels the pictures.
- The student draws a picture of an animal or a person and labels the body parts.

213. Create a word train with small milk cartons. For this activity, the student selects a category (e.g., smell). The topic is taped to the outside of the milk carton. The student lists words that relate to the topic (e.g., skunk, onion, rotten, flowers). If the student is unable to write the words alone, create a word bank and have the student copy the words onto sentence strips. Cut the sentence strips apart, and place them in the milk container. Later, these words may be used to write sentences or incorporated into short paragraphs with one topic sentence.

214. Sentence completion activities may also be used. Give the student sentences that have one word missing. The student fills in the blank. You may provide a choice of two words to insert in the blank, provide a word bank, or, if ready, allow the student to fill in the blank with whatever word he or she would like, as long as it makes sense.

GENERATING IDEAS

Some students have difficulty generating ideas and may need additional prompts and visual aids to get started. This section includes some ideas to help the reluctant writer.

215. Journal writing is a frequently used activity. Because it is not a graded form of writing, there is little risk taking involved for the reluctant writer. Here are several types of journal writing:

- *Question-and-answer journal:* A question is written to the student. The student responds in writing, directing a question back to the adult.
- *Free-response journal:* The student selects and writes freely about a topic. In conjunction with the special education teacher, you help determine an individual goal for the student. The goal may range from writing individual words or a single sentence to filling an entire page.
- *Assigned topics:* These may take various forms. A picture, an object, or perhaps a fill-in-the-blank sentence is provided for the student, and the student responds with one or two sentences.

216. Sequence cards help the student who is unable to generate ideas alone. Provide the student with a sequence of pictures. (If not available in the classroom, these cards may be available from the speech and language clinician.) The student places the cards in sequential order and writes one or more sentences about each picture. If this is too difficult, discuss the first few pictures in the sequence and ask the student to write a sentence about the final picture card only. As the student becomes more proficient, he or she may write about the final two cards and so forth.

If sequence cards are not available, look through the comics section of the newspaper. At times, you may be able to find cartoons with clear pictures that contain three to five picture frames. The frames may be cut apart and used in the same format as sequence cards.

217. Riddles that require a short-answer response are often motivating. On the front of an index card, write some simple riddles. On the back, the student may write the answer to the riddle or (if needed) copy the answer from a model. When the work is complete, the student may practice reading the riddle aloud and share the riddle with the class. As he or she progresses, the student may create his or her own personal riddles. Here are some examples of simple riddles:

- I am thinking of a season of the year when the leaves change color.
- I am thinking of a word that rhymes with *at*, and you can put it on your head.
- I am thinking of an animal that wags its tail and barks.
- I am thinking of an object that you can throw and catch.

218. Reluctant writers often must begin at the basic level. When a student is ready to begin writing sentences, the use of nouns is a perfect place to start. Begin with a simple sentence such as the following "I like" sentences, and then add to the complexity when the student has mastered the skill:

- I like . . . (dogs, ice cream).
- I do not like . . . (peas, work).
- I have a . . . (fish, bike).

When the student is able to fill in the blanks of some basic sentences, he or she can move on to sentences that require more than one word to complete. Examples include the following:

- I like dogs because . . . (they are fun to play with).
- I like my friend because . . . (she is nice).
- After school, I like to . . . (play with my brother).
- I am happy because . . . (I am going to see my grandma).

Once the student is comfortable at this level, the student may begin writing his or her own sentences.

219. Brainstorming helps promote creative thinking and is often used as a prerequisite to writing. There are two simple rules to follow when brainstorming with students. First, there is no right or wrong answer. Second, every answer from a serious idea to an outrageous response is acceptable.

220. Provide detailed instructions for written language assignments. Specific instructions may include the predetermined number of paragraphs or sentences, the overall length, and so on. For example, ask the student to write two paragraphs. Each paragraph should include a topic sentence with two supporting detailed sentences.

Gradually decrease the structure as the student becomes more confident in his or her ability to write.

221. Select a familiar topic. Brainstorm and generate a list of words related to the topic. This becomes the student's word bank, which can be referred to while writing and acts as a springboard for new ideas. It is also a reference for vocabulary and spelling. Once the brainstorming activity is complete, group the words into subtopics. This will help the student organize ideas and write paragraphs. Continue with the same topic for several days.

222. Students who have difficulty generating ideas may need a list of topics from which to choose. **Form 41, Story Starters,** includes some sample ideas that are divided into titles, beginning sentences, and unbelievable excuses. The possibilities are endless. Once the idea is generated, help the student develop an outline of the story or topic. **Form 42, Story Planner,** and **Form 43, Story Outline,** may be used to outline the story.

223. Keep a selection of pictures available for students. Pictures from magazines, posters, newspapers, old photos from antique shops, and others will help the student generate ideas.

224. Some students need a concrete example. Place a common classroom object on the table (e.g., pencil, book, bottle of glue), and ask the student to write a paragraph beginning with "If I were a . . . (pencil, book, bottle of glue), I would. . . ."

225. Ask the student to bring a photo from home and write about the picture. Form 42 can be given to the student who has difficulty organizing his or her thoughts.

226. If the student has difficulty generating ideas, have the student write a minimum number of sentences per day. (You may have to start at one for the student.) Build on the topic each day, and increase the goal each week. Be sure to hold the student responsible for meeting the goal.

227. If the student is unable to generate a sentence without help, write descriptive words or illustrate the idea. Later, combine the words into simple sentences.

228. Write the student's ideas on paper, and ask the student to copy the sentences from the model.

THE WRITING PROCESS

229. Avoid excessive corrections of the mechanical aspects of writing, especially when the student is beginning to write. Focus on the development of ideas.

230. Visual organizers are useful in helping the student define characters, organize thoughts, compare and contrast ideas, and even expand vocabulary. Mapping is one visual organizer. The map should include key ideas and words relating to the topic. Mapping also helps the student visualize the relationship between different parts of the story.

The following example illustrates how to use mapping when writing a simple story. The topic, dogs, is written in the center circle. The paper is divided into four sections. In each section, the student writes words that pertain to some aspect of the topic (e.g., feeding, exercise, grooming, training). When the mapping exercise is complete, the student uses the words to develop sentences or paragraphs. In this example, the student has a main topic and a selection of key words to use for each of four paragraphs.

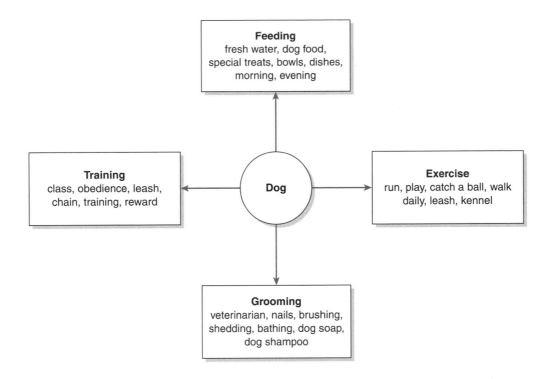

Mapping may also be used to help increase the student's vocabulary. The following is an example of an antonym web map.

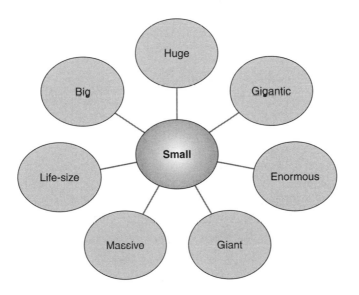

Story characters may also be mapped. For a character map, the main character is listed in the center circle and the individual characteristics are listed in the surrounding circles.

231. Before the student begins to write a story, have the student answer the following questions:

- Who is the main character?
- Who are the other characters in the story?
- What does the main character want to do in the story?
- What happens when the main character does this?
- How does the story end?

These simple questions will help the student organize his or her thoughts and create an outline for the story. Photocopy Form 42 or Form 43 for student use.

232. Teach the importance of including a beginning, a middle, and an end to a paragraph. Transition words help students sequence their thoughts. Incorporate transition words such as *first, next, then, last,* and *finally* when writing paragraphs. Those for more advanced writers may include *accordingly, also, besides, furthermore, nevertheless, otherwise, since, therefore,* and *thus.*

233. Help the student discover the importance of proofreading all assignments. Provide a proofreading checklist that includes the following: capitalization, punctuation, spelling, paragraph indentation, margins, and sentence sense. Have the student read the entire paper and edit it for capital letters. When this is completed, the student checks capitalization off on the form. Then the student reads and edits the paper for punctuation. Continue in this manner until the entire paper is proofread. **Form 44, Proofreading Checklist,** includes several sample checklists that may be reproduced.

234. The SPACE mnemonic (**S**ara **P**icks **A**pples **C**arefully **E**very **A**fternoon) may be used as an error-monitoring strategy when proofreading writing. The acronym stands for the following:

Spelling
Punctuation
Appearance
Capitalization
Error analysis

The student can select the format that is easiest to remember. Practice using the SPACE technique with written language assignments.

235. Ask the student to read his or her story aloud or tape record the story once it is complete. Many students are able to hear erroneous sentence construction even though they do not see it on the paper. It is important when using this method that the student reads the assignment exactly as it is written and does not insert additional words. Give the student ample time to make the corrections.

236. Because written language is an important form of communication, allow students to share their stories and reports often. It is also important for students to hear good models. You may want to ask students to share their stories and reports or select some samples and to read aloud. If a student does not feel comfortable reading aloud, discuss the situation with the supervising teacher. The student may feel more comfortable sharing the story if allowed time to practice reading it prior to sharing.

237. Use a computer or a word processor for some of the written language assignments. Most schools teach keyboarding at a young age. Older students will be able to use the computer to check their spelling and grammar, and to use the thesaurus.

238. Some students may not be able to produce long written assignments; therefore, it may be more important in some cases to look at the quality of the assignment. When teaching topic sentences, details, and closing sentences, ask the student to produce one quality paragraph instead of a series of hastily written paragraphs.

239. When working on class reports, some students may need to use a fill-in-the-blank format. These can easily be created for any topic, and the student can add as many details as required. Here is an example that may be used at the elementary level on the topic of birds:

My bird is a _____. He lives in the _____ part of the United States. He is _____ in color.

240. When writing research papers, students will need help formulating topic sentences and a simple outline, if needed. Encourage the student to look for the details in his or her reading. On the topic of lions, some topic sentences may include the following:

- The lion is a member of the cat family. (The student adds details.)
- The lion can be found in many countries throughout the world. (The student lists the various countries or regions.)
- The lion is a carnivore. (The student lists the food sources.)

For the student who has difficulty reading, you may also want to modify the number of sources in the bibliography.

241. If a student has difficulty organizing thoughts, ask the student to write the first draft on lined notebook paper, skipping several spaces between each sentence. When complete, the student cuts the sentences into strips and physically organizes them. **Form 45, Paragraph Sequencing Activity,** includes sample sentences for the student to use in practicing this technique.

242. The student may be able to present final projects in an alternate format. You may help the student prepare a videotape, demonstration, display, or oral presentation.

SPELLING IN THE CONTEXT OF WRITTEN LANGUAGE ASSIGNMENTS

243. At first glance, a written language assignment with numerous spelling errors may appear to lack creativity and solid ideas. But beginning writers should be allowed to spell phonetically. Ask the student to read the completed assignment to you. Revise the paper with the student. Give encouragement for all attempts.

244. Choose one or more frequently used words from the student's journal or creative writing assignments. Develop a spelling dictionary of frequently misspelled words. Encourage the student to use the dictionary and thesaurus when proofreading assignments.

Students with special needs are often very creative, but a delay in fine motor skills may cause difficulty and frustration when transferring ideas to paper. Instead of allowing the creativity to flow, the student may write in short, choppy sentences to compensate for the difficulty with fine motor control. Interestingly, when the obstacle of writing is removed, many of these students are among the most creative writers.

245. Ask the special or general education teacher to model a correct pencil grip. Check the student's pencil grip. Place adhesive tape or a store-bought pencil grip on the pencil to help the student hold it correctly.

246. Some students are unable to write within the lines of the suggested grade-level paper. If you are working at the upper grades, wide-ruled paper may be secured from primary-level teachers. Students who have difficulty writing within the lines should begin with the wide-ruled paper and slowly graduate to using grade-level paper. If the correct size of paper is unavailable commercially, create the appropriate size for the student using lined paper and a felt-tip pen or by creating it on the computer. Photocopy the paper for future use.

247. Write the student's answers or dictated story in pencil, and ask the student to trace it with a fine-tip pen.

248. It is often difficult for students to copy from a distant model, so provide a close-up model if possible. Students frequently lose their place when transferring information from the board to paper, especially if they are unable to read the material. If the material is written in cursive and the student still prints, you may have to transcribe the material for the student.

249. Affix an alphabet card or alphabet strip to the student's desk or folder so the student is able to see the correct formation of the letters. Allow the use of manuscript or cursive on daily assignments, depending on the student's preference.

250. If appropriate, transcribe long assignments for the student. It may also be permissible for the parent to do this with long homework assignments. If the expectations change, they will need to be communicated to the parent or guardian.

251. If available, provide the student with a word processor or a laptop computer to use for long assignments.

NOTES

12

Spelling

Treat people as if they were what they ought to be and you help them become what they are capable of being.

Johann Wolfgang von Goethe

Spelling words should be compatible with the student's reading level. The special education teacher provides an appropriate list of words if the classroom list is too difficult. As with all modifications, spelling modifications may be simple or complex. Simple ones may include modifying the length of the list, whereas complex ones may include creating an alternate spelling program. If the student is not developmentally ready for a formal spelling program, this time may be used to focus on letter formation and sound–symbol relationships.

GRADE-LEVEL SPELLING LISTS

Many students with disabilities are able to succeed in the regular spelling curriculum with minimal modifications. In conjunction with the supervising teacher, consider some of the following curriculum and instructional modifications:

252. You can often modify a spelling activity by adjusting the number of words on the list. The supervising teacher determines guidelines in accordance with the student's individualized education plan.

253. Once the student has achieved the mastery level on three consecutive tests, increase the goal. For example, the student may study a list of five words for three weeks. If the student successfully masters the list, the goal may increase to seven words. (Frequently it is the paraprofessional's responsibility to track and record the student's progress. When the goal is met, you advise the supervising teacher so that the goal can be

adjusted.) At the beginning of the school year, create a master copy of all of the spelling units. The student will be able to study the words in advance, and if the student forgets the weekly spelling list, he or she has a copy of the comprehensive list at home.

254. Spelling words are often grouped into word families, which are groups of words that have similar endings. By learning the most common word families (see Form 31), the student will be able to spell many different words. The student should begin with simple word patterns with one vowel, such as -at. By learning this simple word pattern, the student will be able to spell the following simple words: *bat, cat, fat, hat, mat, pat, rat,* and *sat.* The student will then be able to proceed to the patterns with more vowels and combinations of consonants.

255. Introduce only one word family at a time. Practice using the pattern until the student is proficient before introducing a new set. For example, on Monday, introduce the -at word family. On Tuesday, review that word family and practice reading the words that were introduced on Monday. If the student clearly recalls the words from the previous lesson, introduce a second word family.

256. Use letter squares from the game Scrabble to reinforce spelling. Or write the word family pattern on an index card, and make individual cards for the initial consonant sounds. The student can manipulate the initial consonant sounds to make new words.

257. If the student is unable to read the spelling list, delete some of the unfamiliar words. Insert commonly used sight words or pattern words that correspond to the current lesson. Ask the special education teacher for an appropriate list of sight words. Form 34 includes the hundred most common words in the English language, which make up almost half of all written material. Words 1–25 on the list make up about one-third of all printed material, so this is a good place to start. Form 33, which lists 220 of the most common sight words by level, is also a helpful resource.

258. If the student is unable to use the current grade-level spelling list, consider using the computer to adapt a previous grade-level list to the format of the current grade-level list.

PARALLEL SPELLING ACTIVITIES

Not all students are developmentally ready for a formalized spelling program. Some students may need parallel activities, such as the following, which may be completed alone, with a peer, or with you.

259. Create a spelling list of initial letter sounds that coincide with the initial letters of the class spelling list. The student can simultaneously work on sound–symbol relationships and letter formation while the other students continue with the class spelling list. During the assessment, the student can write the initial consonant sound as peers write the entire word. Here is an example:

Class	Student
store	s
book	b
take	t

Due to the irregular sounds of words beginning with vowels, there will be times when additional words may need to be substituted. Once the student has mastered the initial consonant sounds, the student may proceed to the final consonants.

260. Start with basic sight words and simple phonetic words such *as, a, at, am,* and *an* when the student is able to reproduce several letter sounds consistently. Form 31 lists common word families, and Column 1 on Form 34 lists some common sight words, which may be incorporated.

261. A simple spelling list may also be created by combining the student's name with several simple sight words. Simple sentences may be developed (written language activity), or the activity may also be used to practice letter formation (fine motor and handwriting activity). Here is an example:

- Weekly spelling list: Mary, my, is, name
- Written language sentences: My name is Mary. Mary is my name.

Once the student has mastered the initial list, names of family members, friends, peers, or pets can be added.

262. Provide supplemental practice pages of the words. The student may trace the words with multiple colors of crayons, felt-tip pens, or fine-tip markers. This approach is good for students who have difficulty learning sounds and need a whole-word method. It also alleviates the frustration of practicing and learning a word incorrectly.

263. Provide practice sheets that the student can trace. Use peers to drill and monitor the student's progress.

DRILL-AND-PRACTICE ACTIVITIES

Drill-and-practice activities take place daily in the classroom. The student may practice alone, with a peer, or with an adult.

264. Group words with common prefixes and suffixes together. The prefix is added at the beginning of a word, and the suffix at the end. Teach the spelling and meaning of the prefixes, suffixes, and base words in isolation. Form 39 contains a list of the most common prefixes and suffixes and their meanings.

265. To help the student visually discriminate between the various parts of the word, use three different colors to highlight the syllables. For example, highlight the base word with yellow, the prefix with green, and the suffix with blue to aid with visual discrimination.

266. Reinforce one spelling rule at a time. Form 32 includes some basic rules that will help students with both spelling and reading. Although not fully inclusive, it has basic guidelines to help get started.

267. Provide a close-up model from which to work. Many students have difficulty copying unknown words from a distant model.

268. Combine spelling and handwriting goals to allow time for extra drill and practice.

269. When practicing spelling words, plan for at least 10 minutes of structured practice time. Students who have trouble with organizational skills will need this time to find and organize their materials.

270. Do not require all students to practice all words daily. This may be too overwhelming for some. Practice two or three words daily if the student is frustrated by a long list.

271. Make supplemental drill-and-practice exercises such as spelling bingo, hangman, and word finds.

272. Vary the daily drill-and-practice exercises. Along with paper-and-pencil tasks, allow daily practice on the chalkboard, in small groups, orally, or with a tape recorder.

273. For younger students, practice spelling words with shaving cream, sand trays, finger paints, or pudding.

274. Provide an audiotape of the word list. To save time, record the pretest while the general education teacher administers it. Once the list is recorded, the student can practice alone, during extra class time, or at home. This tape may also be used if a student needs to retest or was absent during the regular testing session.

275. Make word strips with the spelling words. The student traces each word with three or four colors of markers or crayons. This provides drill and practice for correct letter formation.

276. Allow the student to practice on a typewriter, computer, or word processor.

277. Help the student distinguish between words by outlining spelling words and using configuration clues. The following configuration clues, and the accompanying boxes, are for the words *car* and *boat*. For example, *car* cannot begin with the letter *k* because it would not fit in the box. Boat has a silent letter in the middle because both the *b* and *t* are tall letters, eliminating the possibility of a silent *e* at the end of the word.

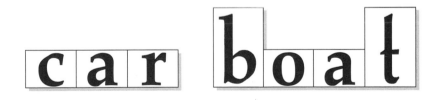

STUDY METHODS FOR SPELLING

For students with disabilities, the most effective method is one that capitalizes on their strengths. The following are guidelines for students who learn visually or auditorily, or who need a multisensory approach for studying spelling. Allow the student to experiment with the various spelling study methods and choose the method that best meets his or her learning style. Practice the method until the student has mastered it. Check the student's work frequently if practicing alone. **Form 46, Study Methods for Spelling,** includes a checklist for each method that can be reproduced for student use.

278. *Visual learners:* This read-and-spell method focuses on students' visual strength and is appropriate for students with hearing impairments or those who rely on visual patterning:

- The student looks at the word while you read it aloud. (Provide the student with a flash card.)
- The student reads the word aloud, spells it aloud, and then reads it again.
- The student attempts to spell the word aloud two times without looking at the card.
- If able to spell the word correctly, the student attempts to write the word without a model.

279. *Auditory learners:* The hear-and-spell method relies heavily on auditory skills to learn new words. Many students learn just by listening. Most students with visual difficulties will also use this method:

- The student observes while the word is written on a flash card, the board, or the overhead projector.
- The student reads the word and repeats the letters verbally after the teacher.
- Once again, the student listens to the teacher spell the word and repeats it after the teacher.
- The student spells the word aloud without assistance.

280. *Multisensory approach:* The cover-and-write method is appropriate for students who need a multisensory approach:

- The student looks at the word and reads it aloud. (Provide flash cards with individual sample words. If the students makes his or her own cards, visually check for accuracy before the student begins the practice session.)
- The student turns the card over (or covers it) and spells the word aloud without looking at it.
- The student writes the word while viewing the model.
- The student compares the word to the model.
- If the word is correct, the student writes the word three additional times without looking at the model.
- A final check is made. If the word is correct, the student practices the next word.

SPELLING TESTS

Many students with disabilities need to learn not only to spell the word, but also to read the word.

281. If the student has difficulty with writing, orally test the student in a quiet area, preferably while peers are taking the written test.

282. Have the student spell the word orally. Write the student's response. This helps the student who experiences fine motor difficulty.

283. Cue the student as to the number of letters in each word when working with silent letters.

284. Test several words daily in place of one final test.

285. Allow a lower-functioning student to select corresponding spelling flash cards for word recognition.

286. If the student needs long periods to process information and you are unable to administer the test individually, create an audiotape. The student will be able to stop the tape and think about the word for as long as needed.

287. If the student reverses letters frequently, ask the student to spell the word orally when correcting the test. Give credit for each correct response.

GRADING

In all instances, the supervising teacher is responsible for selecting grading criteria. You may be asked to keep a record of scores.

288. Record pretest and posttest scores. Give these scores to the classroom teacher, who may base the student's grade on effort and improvement instead of percentiles.

289. Self-monitoring techniques often motivate students. Ask the student to self-monitor spelling progress by creating a chart of his or her pretest and posttest scores.

290. Set a weekly goal. Reward the student if the individual goal is met. All struggling students need encouragement.

NOTES

13

Mathematics

A man has one hundred dollars and you leave him with two—that's subtraction.

Mae West

Mathematics is a second language—the language of symbols. Because mathematics is a process of sequential steps, confusion results when students have difficulty with sequencing. If one step in a process is omitted, students will not arrive at the correct answer. Students who reverse letters may also reverse numbers. Those who are unable to sequence, or have difficulty with memory or auditory and visual processing, usually have difficulty with math. Because new concepts often depend on previously learned skills, students who do not learn the basics of addition, subtraction, or multiplication will have a difficult time with more advanced math concepts. Analyzing the process that students use to complete math problems is important because it helps determine whether they have gaps in learning that need remediation or are skipping various steps of the process.

With basic math, students with disabilities often require the use of concrete materials such as manipulative objects, which aid in the visualization of abstract concepts. Frequently, the math teacher uses manipulative objects to demonstrate a certain skill and for guided practice sessions. Some students may also need manipulative objects for daily assignments. Math is abstract, so manipulative objects help because they can be counted, grouped, and regrouped to arrive at an answer. For some students, using manipulatives with assignments causes confusion because they do not see the connection between the objects and the math problem. Therefore, when working with students in mathematics, first demonstrate and practice with manipulatives. If the students want to continue using the objects, allow them to do so. If they want to proceed without them, that is fine, too. Sometimes the supervising teacher provides training with the manipulative objects. If this is not the case, you can still learn a great amount by observing the direct instruction.

This chapter offers practical ideas to use in supporting students in the area of math. You can refer to the Daily Assignments section in Chapter 9 for additional strategies.

GENERAL TEACHING STRATEGIES

291. Students with disabilities have trouble with abstract concepts. A common comment from students is "Why do we have to learn this?" Discuss how math relates to daily life. Reinforcing math concepts in real-life situations brings meaning and helps students understand the relevance of mathematics. Examples of real-life situations include telling time, measuring sound, understanding budgets, calculating discounts on sale items, balancing a checkbook, counting calories, cooking, reading a bus schedule, determining the amount of rainfall, and so on.

292. Monitoring in mathematics is important. As the student acquires new skills, do not be overly concerned with perfect calculations. First, check for understanding of the process. Once the process is correct, proceed to check the accuracy of the calculations. Limit the number of practice problems to 7–10 per lesson.

293. Reinforce key math terms separately. Provide the student with a dictionary of math terms taken directly from the math textbook. Help the student create drawings and systematic examples to illustrate the various concepts.

294. Use drawings, diagrams, and visual demonstrations to help the student establish the relationship between the concrete and the abstract. When problem solving is involved, encourage the student to illustrate the possible solutions.

295. Use colored chalk or fine-tip markers when reinforcing assignments. Direct the student's attention to the important points. Color-code groups of ones, tens, and hundreds, or color-code the columns of numbers to help with regrouping.

296. Highlight the similar math operations on each page (e.g., addition problems in yellow, subtraction problems in blue). If the assignment includes several types of math calculations, such as addition and subtraction, on one page, the student should complete all the addition problems before proceeding to the subtraction problems.

297. Teach math fact families. Show the student the relationships between numbers. Here is an example:

$6 + 4 = 10$	$10 - 4 = 6$
$4 + 6 = 10$	$10 - 6 = 4$

298. If applicable, model math problems using manipulatives. The special or general education teacher can demonstrate the correct procedure. When modeling, explain each step verbally. Then instruct the student to verbalize each step to you while practicing the procedure. Listen carefully. You will be able to understand the student's thinking process and analyze which step is causing difficulty. Patterns of errors usually emerge in the following areas: inadequate knowledge of facts, incorrect operations, and use of ineffective strategies.

299. When using a number line to reinforce concepts, create it on the floor with masking tape. To aid with directionality, the student may walk on the number line. If the student is unable to grasp the number line concept, use counters, cubes, popsicle sticks, or buttons.

300. When teaching the concept of money, use real money instead of paper or cardboard money.

301. For students who have difficulty counting coins, try coding the coins. To do this activity, the student must be able to count by fives. With fingernail polish, paint one red dot on each nickel, two red dots on each dime, and five red dots on each quarter. Each dot represents five, so the student counts by fives and adds the remaining pennies at the end. For example:

one quarter	+	one dime	+	one nickel	+	two pennies
5, 10, 15, 20, 25		30, 35		40		41, 42

302. Test the student individually. If the student is required to take timed tests, reduce the number of problems or increase the time limit. Provide additional paper to diagram or draw pictures if the basic facts have not been memorized.

An alternative to traditional timed tests is to use the computer. With many commercial math programs, a time limit and number of problems may be preset.

Some classroom teachers insist on using timed tests, although for students with disabilities the most frequent outcome of timed tests is frustration. Ask the student to graph the results, and encourage the student to look for improvement.

303. Simplify vocabulary with reinforcing word problems. Often, word problems include irrelevant information. Discuss why the information is irrelevant. Cross it out. Teach key words that are associated with word problems. When reinforcing word problems, it is helpful to ask the student to do the following:

a. Read the problem, and determine the question.
b. Reread the word problem, looking for key words such as *altogether, together, in all, are left, spent,* and *remain.*
c. Draw a picture of the word problem.
d. Write out the problem. Estimate the answer before solving it. If the answer seems reasonable, solve the problem.

304. The following strategies are appropriate for solving word problems. Demonstrate how to use these skills:

- Estimate the answer.
- Make a guess and check the answer.
- Look for a pattern.
- Draw a picture of the problem.
- Work the problem backward.
- Make a list.
- Create a chart or a table.
- Break the problem into smaller parts.

305. Draw pictures and create memory tricks. Ask the student to do some, too. Here are a couple of examples:

Long division: This family list will help the student remember the steps to long division.
Step 1: DAD—divide
Step 2: MOM—multiply

Step 3: SISTER—subtract
Step 4: BROTHER—bring down

Fractions: When dividing fractions, teach students the simple phrase **K**ids **C**an **R**un.
Keep the first fraction.
Change the sign from divide to multiply.
Reverse the last fraction.

PARALLEL MATH ACTIVITIES

Some students are unable to complete the same curriculum as the rest of the class. For these students, it is important to be aware of the goals and objectives written in their individualized education plan (IEP). Supplementary skills that correspond with the class activity can be provided in the classroom. Listed below are several activities that can be completed with the student.

306. Provide parallel activities in the same content areas as those used by the rest of the class, and use the same manipulatives. For example, if the class is learning addition with regrouping, the student may work on basic addition facts. It is therefore possible for the student to still be involved in the discussion and demonstration.

307. Correlate the objectives from the IEP with the instruction. If the student is working on number recognition, use daily assignments or the textbook to find numbers. If the objective is number formation, the student can copy problems from the textbook.

308. Use dot-to-dot activities for number sequencing and number recognition.

309. Work on number formation with the use of tracers or templates.

310. Provide the student with number cards. Work on the chronological sequencing of numbers. The same cards may be used for one-to-one correspondence, ordering from least to greatest, and number recognition.

311. Make cards for numbers and mathematical symbols. Have the student put them together into correct mathematical equations. The student may copy the equations onto paper.

312. Collect shells, beads, seeds, various shapes of pasta, and buttons. Put them into boxes or bags, and use these collections to sort and classify objects. The materials may also be used to assist with one-to-one correspondence.

313. Use egg cartons to sort materials and to establish the concept of a group. This concept needs to be established before addition and subtraction can be introduced.

314. Teach the student the functions of a calculator, and allow the student to do some of the problems from the textbook with it.

315. The student may collate the class's math papers into order based on math pages, units, and so on.

316. When providing a parallel math curriculum, coordinate the student's assessments, seatwork, and rewards with the general education class.

317. Look for educational games the student can play with other students in the classroom. *EducationalLearningGames* (www.educationallearninggames.com) provides a list of commercial games searchable by subject. These include math cards and board games for shapes, counting, place value, measurement, percentages, and many more.

318. If a computer is available, look for computer programs that include number recognition, counting, matching, dot-to-dot, or sequencing of numbers. Most schools have a wide assortment of computer games. Talk to the technology specialist to see what is available.

319. Keep a box of supplemental math materials for students who need reinforcement. With activities related directly to the current lesson, the activities can be used when the student has a few minutes of free time. Activities can be selected daily from the box, and materials updated as needed.

320. Do you need to brush up on math skills? There will be times when you are expected to help a student in area such as algebra or geometry and you have no clue how to do it. Go to www.math.com and click on the Parents section. Developed for parents to help their kids, it is a great resource for brushing up on skills before supporting students.

MODIFYING MATH ASSIGNMENTS

321. Place arrows on the student's worksheet to assist with directionality. Students often try to perform math calculations from left to right instead of right to left, which is required for many math calculations.

322. Draw dotted lines between columns of math problems so the student is able to record the information in the correct column. Lined paper turned vertically creates ready-made columns, or graph paper may be used for instant organization.

323. Box in the ones column so that the student begins math calculations from the right-hand column.

324. Check to see if consumable texts are available. A student with fine motor difficulty will not have to copy the problems; therefore, the student will be able to spend more time with the actual calculations.

325. If consumable texts are unavailable, ask permission to photocopy and enlarge the text so the student may write on the photocopied page.

326. When working with problem-solving activities, emphasize the steps, not the final answer. Many students do not participate in problem-solving activities for fear that the final computation will be incorrect.

327. Number the steps in word problems, and highlight important words.

328. Allow the student to use charts, graphs, and tables to complete the assignments once the processes of addition, subtraction, multiplication, and division are understood.

329. When using addition or multiplication charts, provide the student with a cutout L. This will help the student find the intersection box of columns and rows.

330. Give the student ample time to memorize the math facts before using the calculator. If able to count by two, five, and ten, the student may also learn to count by three, four, six, and so on, which will enable him or her to multiply without the use of a calculator.

331. Touch Math is a program that provides hands-on learning without the use of manipulatives. Touch-points are strategically located on each number, and the student counts the points. The students who is able to count both forward and backward can easily learn to add and subtract. The program also uses touch-points for multiplication and division.

STUDENT AIDS

332. When teaching multistep math calculations, provide a visual model next to the written steps so the student can see the correlation between the model and the written problem.

333. Create a math reference booklet that includes the basic math concepts covered in class, the terminology, and a visual diagram for each step. The student can refer to the booklet if confused about a mathematical operation.

334. Attach a number line to the student's desk. This will help the student with addition, subtraction, and the correct formation of numbers. It will also assist students who have trouble with number reversals.

335. Teach the student how to use the classroom's face clock as a math tool. The student can count for addition and subtraction facts to 12. This will support the student who is averse to having a number line placed on the desk.

336. Create a chart with two number lines. Label one for addition with an arrow pointing to the right, and the other for subtraction with an arrow pointing to the left. This will help the student internalize the concept.

337. Allow the student to use rubber number stamps if number formation is extremely difficult.

338. Use stick-on notes to help the student keep his or her place in the text.

NOTES

14

Classroom Assessments

There is no failure except in no longer trying.

Elbert Hubbard

Classroom assessments may be modified in two ways. The supervising teacher may modify the content of an assessment based on a student's individualized education plan (IEP), or the student may need instructional modifications when taking the actual test. As a paraprofessional, some of your assessment-related responsibilities may include monitoring the student during the assessment, reading the test aloud, recording the student's answers, or helping the student organize his or her thoughts and ideas. Often, students require alternate forms of assessment due to difficulties with reading and written language. If the goal is to measure the student's knowledge of a curriculum area, it is important to test only that area and not to penalize the student for the disability.

GENERAL STRATEGIES

339. Test orally instead of requiring the student to write the answers on paper.

340. Allow the student to demonstrate mastery of the concept being tested by making an illustration or creating a final project.

341. Write the student's answers to the questions. Be sure to record the answers verbatim.

342. Allow the student extra time to complete the test. Administer the test outside the classroom area if possible, in a place that is free of distracting stimuli.

343. When supervising tests, especially those that have time constraints, ask the student to first complete the items about which he or she is confident of the answer before returning to the more difficult test items.

344. Read all test directions orally. Check for understanding.

345. Tape record the test, and allow the student to record his or her answers verbally.

346. Maintain a record of the pretests and posttests. These records will reflect the student's effort and improvement. The scores should be given to the special education teacher.

347. If a test contains multiple parts, be sure that each specific section includes a set of directions. Point out the various sections, and be sure the student understands the individual instructions.

348. Ask the student to circle, underline, or highlight key words in the directions. Or you may do this before handing the test to the student.

349. Emphasize recognition of facts rather than factual recall on tests. If you encounter trick questions on commercially made tests, point these out to the supervising teacher. The teacher can make a decision as to whether or not to delete the question.

350. If the district requires the student to take standardized tests, ask if it is possible to order consumable tests. This will eliminate the need to transfer the student's responses to a computer scorecard. If a computer scorecard must be used, have the student complete the test on paper; then you can record the answers when the student finishes.

TYPES OF ASSESSMENTS

The following assessments are the most common paper-and-pencil tests used in the classroom environment. Some of the common instructional modifications are listed for each test.

351. *Essay tests:* These are often the most difficult types of test for students with special needs. These involve reading and understanding the question, recollecting information, organizing thoughts, and transferring that information to paper. The following will help you assist the student with essay tests:

- First, be certain the student understands the test question. Check for understanding by asking the student to paraphrase the question.
- Be certain the student understands the following words that regularly appear in the directions for essay tests: *compare, contrast, explain, describe, list.*
- Help the student create a simple outline so that the student can organize and sequence his or her thoughts before writing.
- If allowed, provide a list of the key vocabulary words that the student can include in the essay. If there are additional words the student would like you to list (e.g., words that are difficult to spell), also list these.
- You may be asked to write the student's responses to the essay questions. If so, be sure to record them verbatim.

352. *Fill in the blank:* For this type of test, a word bank is frequently provided. If not, ask if one may be created for the student. Before testing, ask the student to read each word in the word bank and to recall as much information as possible about the individual

words. If a word bank is used during the assessment, the student should draw a light pencil mark through the response in case it needs to be changed later.

353. *Matching:* If the matching list is long, check to see whether the list may be divided into groups. This must be done under the direction of the supervising teacher because as selections are decreased it automatically increases the odds of the student receiving a higher grade. Matching tests often contain clues within the sentence structure. Help the student become aware of this. For example, if the beginning part of the sentence in column A is very long, odds are that the second part in column B may be one of the shorter answers. If the first part of the sentence ends with the word *an,* the second part of the sentence will begin with a word that has an initial vowel sound. General education students often easily grasp simple strategies such as these, but the student with special needs may be so intent on trying to read the material that the obvious clues are often missed.

354. *Multiple choice:* When taking a multiple-choice test, the student should first read the entire test and answer the questions for which he or she definitely knows the answers. Once this step is complete, the student should read the questions a second time, answering the questions that are familiar. With the remainder of the questions, the student should narrow the choices by first eliminating all answers that make no sense. When this is complete, the student will need to make educated guesses. On multiple-choice tests, it is often the case that the answer to a given question may be found in the context of other questions throughout the test. Therefore, encourage the student to read the entire test very carefully.

355. *Short answer:* These tests are very similar to essay tests. First, be sure that the student understands the test questions. Check for understanding of the direction words (*compare, contrast, explain, describe, list*) before starting the test. If appropriate, supply the student with a list of vocabulary words applicable to the unit.

356. *Standardized tests:* Many standardized tests rely heavily on the student's ability to read the material. If the student's reading level is several years below grade level, this will be a frustrating experience. Because there are strict guidelines for administering standardized tests, they cannot be modified. Another area of concern with standardized testing is that the response sheet is often computer scored, and students frequently lose their place when filling in the corresponding circles. If the student must take the test, one option is to use a consumable test booklet. If that is not available, the answers need to be transferred to the computer scorecard when the test is complete.

The special education team will address standardized testing. If the student is excused from standardized testing, which will be reflected in the IEP, use the time for review, reteaching of materials, or a preview of upcoming lessons.

357. *True/false:* This type of test is often difficult for students because the test questions frequently contain double negatives. If you encounter this type of question, ask the supervising teacher if you may rephrase it.

NOTES

15

Behavior Management

Punish the incident and treat the problem.

Anonymous

Personal behavior is hard to change. Take a moment to think about your own life. Are there things you would like to change but haven't because it is too difficult? Have you put off starting a daily exercise program because it is just too hard to fit into your schedule or it seems like too much work? As an adult, you have control over whether or not you choose to make these personal changes. Students struggle with the same issues with personal change. Their behaviors, although not acceptable in the school setting, may be accepted at home, and they have had a great deal of time to develop and practice ways to avoid difficult situations. For most students, however, behaviors are learned, and learned behaviors can be changed with patience, persistence, and positive reinforcement.

Why do students misbehave? Frequently, misbehavior from students with special needs is a cover-up for lack of success in the school environment. By acting out, they avoid the embarrassment of being perceived as "dumb." Students may act out with the intention of being removed from the classroom, therefore avoiding the assignment that they were unable to complete. Students may also develop an "I don't care" attitude to avoid work that they are incapable of doing. Therefore, students who struggle often have to make a choice between looking like a bad kid (which is often perceived by their peers as "cool") or looking dumb in front of their peers. For many, the choice is an easy one.

So, as professionals, what do we do? We try to help these students become capable and successful in the classroom environment by modifying and adapting the curriculum so that they can succeed. At times, we also try to control the negative behavior by threatening, removing privileges, and contacting parents. This may work for some students, but for many, the options soon are used up and there is nothing else left to try.

When working with a student who misbehaves, patience is essential. Being patient and calm decreases the possibility that you will reinforce the student's negative behavior. Staying calm also decreases the chance that you may respond out of anger and frustration, perhaps saying or doing something that you will later regret. Persistence is necessary because the student must learn that there are consistent consequences for his or her actions. The consequence for a specific behavior that occurs on Monday should be the same consequence if the behavior is repeated on Tuesday, Wednesday, Thursday, or Friday. If you are not persistent and consistent, the student may continually repeat the behavior to see if he or she is able to get away with it.

It is also imperative to respond to the student positively. This may seem ironic when discussing misbehavior, but it is important to "catch" the student in appropriate, responsible situations. Some students act out for attention. For these students, you need to find situations when they are acting responsibly so that you can compliment them and provide positive feedback. Conversely, there are times when it may be appropriate to ignore the inappropriate behavior if doing so may result in a decrease in the negative behavior.

The behavior of some students is so severe that a specific behavior plan needs to be implemented. Many of these students take medication to help control their behavior. The supervising teacher will explain how to implement behavior plans and what to do when a situation is out of control and backup support is needed. The behavior plan developed by the special education team overrides the information presented in this section.

As a paraprofessional, you will work with students who have behavior difficulties. Therefore, it is important to anticipate and discuss specific situations with the supervising teacher in advance. Some basic questions can be found in **Form 47, "What Do I Do if . . . ?"**

BEHAVIOR STRATEGY TIPS

358. View misbehavior as a teachable moment. After an incident has occurred and the student is calm, discuss the behavior with the student and determine alternate forms of release. **Form 48, Behavior Change Plan,** may be filled out in conjunction with the student, or the student may fill it out alone. In place of the form, the student may answer the following questions on a piece of paper that should be given to the supervising teacher for follow-up:

Form 48: Sample Behavior Change Plan

What happened? (list the incident that occurred)	What happened before the incident? (list the activity, subject, or any helpful information)	How did I respond?	What are some alternate responses if this situation reoccurs?
I was kicked out of class.	Nothing. I was trying to do my work. John kept turning around and bugging me.	I threw my pencil at him and told him to shut his mouth.	I could try to ignore him. I suppose I could go sit somewhere else.
Additional support needed or comments. Talk to the classroom teacher and ask if there is an alternative place to sit if I cannot get my work done in my assigned seat.			

- What happened?
- What happened before the incident?
- What was your response?
- How could you respond differently if the situation reoccurs?
- How can I help you? What do you need?

359. Avoid power struggles with the student. You will not gain anything.

360. When dealing with a difficult student, remain calm and speak in a quiet, calm voice. Be aware of your body language.

361. Do not get backed into a corner by making empty threats that you are not prepared to follow through on. You will lose credibility quickly.

362. Do not give in to anger. If you feel you are losing control, it may be best to walk away. Often the student wants your attention, and removing yourself from the situation no longer provides an audience for the student.

363. Do not take student comments personally. When a student acts out, you may be accused of being unfair, unreasonable, or worse. Keep in mind that these comments would be directed to any person of authority.

364. Take time to think before responding. Count to 10, take several deep breaths, and think about your response before actually saying it. After pausing to think, you may decide that the best response is no response at all.

365. Select your battles carefully. Some of the small battles are just not worth it. Ask your supervising teacher which issues are the most important and which ones can perhaps be overlooked.

366. Offer acceptable choices to the student, but think through them first because you will need to live with them. If in doubt, explain to the student that you need some time to think, and then discuss the issue with the supervising teacher.

367. Ignore the student. Often the student has determined exactly what will push your buttons. If this is the case, try to ignore the student as long as his or her action is not harmful or hurtful to others.

368. Proximity control is often used in the classroom. Stand or sit close to the student.

369. Some students do not realize that their habits are annoying to others. These habits may include continually blurting out answers, tapping a pencil on the desk, fidgeting with small items, and so on. Create a visual signal to let the student know it is occurring and should stop.

370. Often, taking a short walk in the hall is enough to calm the student and avoid a possible explosive situation.

371. Humor can often defuse a situation. However, if you are not by nature a funny person, do not try to experiment with humor during a crisis. More than likely, the student will take it as sarcasm because it is out of character.

372. Some students have a very low frustration threshold and tend to lash out when frustrated. If you notice that a student is becoming extremely frustrated with an assignment or an activity, take a break and try it later.

373. Often, students can sense when their behaviors are escalating to the point of no return. If a student is aware that an outburst is about to occur, he or she may need some time away from the classroom. Arrange a location free of stimulus where the student may go. This may be a counselor's office, the library, or any suitable quiet area in the classroom environment. This option should be listed in the student's individualized education plan.

374. There may be times when a student is unable to calm down and refuses to leave the setting. If this happens, you may have to remove the other students from the situation and call for support. If the situation is potentially dangerous, be sure to remove from the area all objects that the student could use to harm himself or herself or others.

375. Do not expect changes to occur overnight. For some chronic misbehavior, you may have to correct, correct, and correct again. Change takes time. You may wonder how many times it will take to correct the behavior. The only answer is "as long as it takes."

376. As a paraprofessional, you may be asked to gather and document information in the classroom. The supervising teacher may ask you to target specific behaviors. A target behavior is one that can be seen, is measurable, and is well defined. Some examples include following the teacher's direction within 10 seconds, not arguing, following classroom rules, being on task 80 percent of the time, and being on time to class.

377. When attention is focused on a target behavior for the student with special needs, it is easy to overlook the fact that the same behavior occurs frequently with students in the general population. A simple way to compare the target behavior of a specific student to that of peers is to use a tally sheet. To tally information, you will need to have a watch or clock with a second hand. **Form 49, Tally Sheet,** is a reproducible form that you can use to record the data. Student 1 is the target student. Select two or three other students in the classroom for comparison. For the following hypothetical example, every 30 seconds you would glance at one of the students (Student 1, 2, then 3, in consecutive order) and make a mark if the student is on task. At the end of the observation time, you will have a good indicator of the student's on-task behavior in relation to his or her peers. The tally sheet may also be used to document behavior for an individual student.

Form 49: Sample Tally Sheet

Student	Date/Time	Observable Behavior
	March 10 9:00–9:15 am	On-task behavior during independent work time (30-second intervals)
	Tally Space	
Student 1 (target student)	**Total**	
Student 2 (peer)	**Total**	
Student 3 (peer)	**Total**	

378. Another option is to videotape the entire class and tally the target behaviors while viewing the video. This makes it easy to assess and document more than one target behavior at a time. The video is confidential and should be erased once the observation is complete. Its only purpose is observation.

379. Consistency is important. Do not be lenient and easygoing on days when you feel good and then harsh on days when you feel tired or stressed.

380. If you want the student to do something, use statements and not questions. For example, if it is time for the student to clear off his or her desk, say, "Please put your things away now." Do not ask, "Would you like to put away your things?" You may not like the reply.

381. Before giving a direction, be sure to have the student's attention. Look for eye contact. Give only one or two directions at a time.

REINFORCEMENT AND DISCIPLINE

382. If the student consistently needs to be disciplined during a specific academic class, it is important to determine whether the current modifications are appropriate. Report this to the supervising teacher. Do not wait until the situation escalates.

383. If a student disrupts the class frequently, report the behavior to the special education teacher. No student is allowed to interfere with the education of the other students. An alternative for the student who repeatedly disrupts the class is to video-tape the lesson. The student can watch the video during the next class session and complete the assignment alone or with you. The student returns to the class when the assignment or lesson is complete. In this way, the student is still held responsible for the assignment. For many students who act out, positive reinforcement comes from the other students. When the student is removed from the classroom, the audience is no longer available.

384. At times, a student needs a place to get away from stimuli to regroup. Find a quiet place for the student in the classroom, in another classroom, or in a vacant area. Give the student a special pass to use in this situation. If the area is in another classroom, a telephone code may be worked out with the cooperating teacher. One ring means the student is on the way. If the student does not arrive, the cooperating teacher can call back. The student may take class work and complete it in this area. Rules must be set. Here are a few examples:

- The work area may be used only during class work times.
- A pass must be obtained from the classroom teacher when leaving the classroom.
- You must return within a specified number of minutes.

Often, students with behavior disorders are more dependent on external reinforce-ment than others in their peer group are. In an inclusive setting, students may need con-stant reassurance that they are doing well. A reward system may help meet this need in the classroom. Reward systems are also used frequently in the cafeteria, during study periods, or at recess.

Reward systems must be implemented cautiously. Their purpose is to help the student improve behavior. The positive feedback that a student receives for behaving appropriately should be the final reward. As a result, the outcome of all reward systems is to eliminate the tangible reward.

So when a reward system is used, the focus is on positive verbal feedback and the tan-gible reward should be secondary. Positive comments should be emphasized with the student before you actually give the reward. Let us look at an example. Jerry's goal is to stay on task for increments of 15 minutes. When he meets this objective, an appropriate comment would be, "Jerry, you certainly have been working hard. Show me what you have finished." Once you have checked and commented on the assignment, you may give the reward.

There are many types of reward systems. Before deciding on which one to use, it is important to establish a list of reinforcement activities or rewards for the student. Some examples of rewards include extra computer time, time to chat with friends, choosing a friend for a special activity, omission of a homework assignment (at the teacher's discretion), or something as simple as being the first student in line. Be sure that the supervising teacher approves the list of reinforcements.

Once the reinforcements have been approved, the supervising teacher will help determine how the day should be divided and how the reward system will be implemented. If the target behavior for the student is to stay on task during independent work time, feedback may be required every 5 to 10 minutes. If the target behavior is to complete and return daily assignments, a chart may be used only during the morning check-in. The supervising teacher will provide clear guidelines as to when and why the points will be awarded.

385. You can use charts to record the student's behavior. As you walk around the class, place a check mark or a sticker on the chart for appropriate behavior and work completion. When the chart is full, it may be turned in for a reward. Some examples are included on **Form 50, Sample Reinforcement Charts**. These are very generic and may be adapted to meet the student's individual needs. For younger students, cute and colorful charts with matching stickers may be purchased from teacher supply stores.

386. For older students, a simple positive reinforcement phrase or a pat on the back can be sufficient reinforcement.

387. Keep parents informed when the student has shown improvement during the day. Create a list of positive sayings, such as the following:

Awesome day!
I discovered the secret to success today!
Superstar!
I am a great student!
Wow!

More sayings can be found on **Form 51, Positive Reinforcement Phrases,** which you can photocopy onto fluorescent paper or an 8½" x 11" full label sheet so that students may stick it on their notebooks or folders. Cut the phrases apart, and place them in an envelope. When the student has a good day, the student can select a phrase strip to take home. If proper guidelines are set, older students will be able to monitor their own progress. Rewards may be given when the student has received a specific number of positive phrases. This is a simple way to communicate with the parents. Some parents may also offer an incentive at home.

388. You may implement a point system and assign points, ranging from zero to three, to each class block. The supervising teacher will determine the guidelines for receiving the points. **Form 52, Point Sheet,** may be reproduced to keep track. Homework assignments can be included on the sheet, and there is a space for positive comments. At the end of the week, points are tallied and the student receives a predetermined reward if the individual goal has been met. This is appropriate for older students.

389. A token system works well for many students. The tokens may be small laminated paper shapes, buttons, beads, or whatever else might be easy to keep in your possession. Tokens may be distributed randomly to the student for appropriate behavior. The student keeps the tokens in a container, and when the student has a predetermined number of tokens, they may be exchanged for rewards. If the "cost" of the rewards varies, encourage the student to set long-term goals and save tokens until a goal is achieved.

390. Tokens may also be used in the reverse. The student receives a set number of tokens upon arrival in the morning and then returns a token every time he or she exhibits an inappropriate behavior. At the end of the day, the student may use the remainder of the tokens for a reward. When using this method, be sure that the student clearly understands the rules before beginning. The rules should be specific and in writing. A rule such as "Respect others" is hard to enforce. Therefore, it is better to write clear and concise rules such as "Do not talk when others are talking," "Wait until you are called on before answering," and "Do not take other people's belongings."

391. The class discipline plan may not be appropriate for all students. Some students may need a supplemental discipline plan with extra warnings coupled with a reward system. Some students should only receive one warning, or else they might take advantage of the system. Other students may need several. The supervising teacher will provide the supplemental discipline plan. All adults involved should be aware of the plan and follow it.

392. A daily report can be used to monitor behavior and academic goals. An easy way to create a daily report is to tape an index card to the student's desk. Subjects are added to the card throughout the day. For younger students, a happy face may be placed on the card next to the subject if the student has experienced success during the time block. For older students, a rating scale of zero to three may be used. Form 52 may be used for older students and sent home daily to increase communication between the school and the home.

393. A daily log has proven successful in coordinating home and school communication. It is usually a spiral notebook that remains in the backpack. Both parents and teachers use this log to write comments, concerns, and suggestions. The student is rewarded for taking home and returning the notebook daily.

394. Teach the student to use positive self-talk. "I can do this!" "I can handle this!" or "I'm good at this!" are all examples of this. If you hear a student using negative self-talk or putting himself or herself down, stop the student and help him or her rephrase the comments positively.

ATTENTION DEFICIT DISORDER AND ATTENTION DEFICIT HYPERACTIVITY DISORDER

Some students with disabilities are also medically diagnosed as having attention deficit disorder (ADD) or attention deficit hyperactivity disorder (ADHD). Modifications need to be made within the classroom setting if these students are to experience success in school. For the majority of these students, the strategies and modifications discussed previously in this book will be helpful in the classroom. The strategies in this section pertain directly to those who have trouble with attention, on-task behavior, impulsivity, or distractibility.

Not all students with a medical diagnosis of ADD or ADHD receive services under the umbrella of special education. To receive services, they must have a primary handicapping condition that meets federal guidelines for special education. Some students, but not all, are served under the category of Other Health Impairments. Those who do not receive special education services may receive support in the classroom under a 504 Plan. If this is the case, the supervising teacher is the general education teacher and the special education department is not directly involved with the services for these students.

PROVIDING STRUCTURE FOR STUDENTS

395. Daily structure needs to be provided for all students, but for these students it is especially important. Transition times are difficult and should be closely monitored. If the general education teacher does not have a daily schedule posted, create one for the student. Discuss the schedule, and point out daily changes in advance.

396. Provide a visual cue to the student several minutes before a transition is to occur. The student may need extra time to adjust and organize materials before beginning a new subject. Provide extra structure during transition times. Many students tend to get into trouble during transition times, so monitor these times closely.

397. Review the classroom rules frequently. If the student is having difficulty with a specific rule, write down the rule. Be clear and concise. The student cannot argue with a piece of paper. Give specific examples of the rule, such as sitting quietly while the teacher is talking, staying in your seat when the teacher is talking, or sharpening pencils at the beginning of the class period.

398. Always state the positive action you would like to see from the student. For example, if the student is running in the hall, simply say, "Walk, please."

399. Check-in and check-out times are important for the student. Go to the student's classroom, and use this time to check homework and assignment books or to remind the student to turn in completed projects and assignments.

WORKING WITH STUDENTS

400. Make sure you have the student's attention when talking to him or her. You may have to ask the student to physically stop the current activity to get his or her attention.

401. Include the student in small-group activities and instruction whenever possible. Immediate feedback is important.

402. Provide one- or two-step directions only. Check for understanding by asking the student to repeat each direction back to you.

403. Give one assignment at a time. Many students with ADD or ADHD are overwhelmed easily. Keep all assignments in a folder. If the student falls behind, have the student complete some of the assignments orally to catch up.

404. Allow ample time for hands-on instruction. This will help actively engage the student in the learning process. Active participation is extremely important because it helps the student remain focused.

405. Modify daily assignments to alleviate frustration. (See the Daily Assignments section in Chapter 9.)

406. Use computer instruction for academic reinforcement when appropriate. The computer provides immediate feedback, self-paced instruction, and increased motivation.

407. Use a timer to assist the student with on-task behavior. Explain the task you would like the student to complete, and then set the timer for the specified amount of time. Start with a short assignment that the student can successfully complete. Longer assignments may be divided into sections. Once the student is able to stay on task for the specified amount of time, increase the time by one or two minutes.

408. Allow the student time during the day to get up, walk around, and stretch. It may be appropriate for the student to sit in the back of the classroom so he or she is able to stand or sit as needed with minimal disruption to the class. If movement is necessary, provide clear guidelines about when it is appropriate.

409. Many students benefit from immediate feedback. Provide self-correctors so the student is able to correct his or her own assignments as they are completed. For example, once five math problems have been completed, allow the student to correct the problems before proceeding to the next group.

410. Students often have difficulty making decisions. When appropriate, allow the student to choose between two or three activities. In this manner, tasks are still completed, but the student is allowed a small amount of control.

WORKING WITH IMPULSIVE AND EASILY DISTRACTED STUDENTS

411. Seat the student in a location with limited visual stimuli. Artwork or cluttered walls may distract the student from lessons.

412. Check seating arrangements. Students should not be seated near doors, windows, or high-traffic areas.

413. Give the student extra time to complete assignments, even if the assignments have been modified.

414. Timed activities and tests should be avoided. Students may become frustrated when others have completed the assignment. Frequently, the student guesses on the remainder or gives up. Discuss alternate activities with the supervising teacher.

415. Teach the student to stop and think before responding. Create a visual signal between you and the student. For example, place your finger aside your nose; when the student observes this, he or she will know that it is time to slow down and think about the action.

416. Use visual clues for movement. A simple technique is to place one red and one green cup within the student's sight. Stack the cups. When the red cup is on top, the student must remain seated. When the green cup is on top, the student may move about the classroom. This can also be done using red and green construction paper.

417. Teach the student positive self-talk. Often, students are heard using negative self-talk. Try to reverse this to positive self-talk. The student may say "I can do this" repeatedly. For some students, repeating the directions aloud is especially helpful when complex steps and directions are given. It will also help the student remain focused on the current task.

418. If possible, seat the student near quiet, independent workers who are good role models. Do not seat disruptive or easily distracted students together.

419. Allow the student to have only the necessary materials for the current assignment on top of the desk. Toys and play objects should remain at home. If the student must have something, give him or her a small piece of clay, a small balloon filled with flour, or a stress ball to squeeze.

NOTES

A Final Note From the Author

The paraprofessional's job is essential to every inclusive setting. In school districts nationwide, the number of paraprofessionals is equal to or exceeds the number of special education teachers. Whether you work several hours a day or are employed as a full-time employee, you are a vital part of the program. Inclusive settings cannot exist without your support.

Not everyone can be a paraprofessional. The job is very demanding. You may be required to work with many students and teachers throughout the day, and this requires extreme flexibility on your part. Communication skills are important; a positive attitude, enthusiasm, and patience are also crucial for success.

Though the job is demanding, the rewards are numerous! They might include the dazzling smile of a student who has just learned to read or the sparkle of success in the eyes of a child who is unable to communicate verbally. Maybe it will be the voices of encouragement from classmates when a student is faced with a difficult challenge or simply knowing that your job makes a positive difference in the lives of your students. Without your support, inclusive settings would cease to exist.

Whether you are thinking about applying for a job, were recently hired, or are an experienced paraprofessional, I hope this book will provide you with the support you need.

I wish you luck. You will make a difference in the lives of many.

Peggy Hammeken

Resources

Reproducible Forms

Form 1

Contact List

Name and Position	Contact Information	Notes

Form 2

Discussion Activities for Paraprofessionals

The general education teacher asks you to go to the office and pull the confidential files for some of the students in her math class. You do not work with these students.

In the classroom, you overhear a group of students making negative comments about one of the students you support in the classroom.

The classroom teacher asks you to contact the parents about discipline problems that have occurred during the day.

The supervising general education teacher consistently leaves the classroom, leaving you in charge of all the students.

You feel that your supervising general education teacher treats several students in an unprofessional manner. You do not want to approach him, so you decide to discuss the situation with some of your colleagues.

Your own child has just been diagnosed with ADD. Several students whom you work with have learning disabilities and are also diagnosed as having ADD. You want to find out the types of medication and the dosage that these students take. You decide to talk to the nurse about these children.

You attend a party at a friend's house and discover that the parents of a student you support are also at the party. The parents start asking you about their child's progress. Later, your friend asks you for specifics about the child.

Part of your job description includes helping a student who uses a wheelchair to get through the lunch line and get situated at a table. While the student is eating, you monitor the lunchroom and chat with students. While roving throughout the lunchroom, you hear a group of girls discussing someone who has been sexually assaulted.

Form 3, Page 1

Job Description

Classroom: _____   Time: _____

Behavior Management

- ☐ help students stay on task
- ☐ collect data and document behaviors
- ☐ maintain daily logs or journals
- ☐ manage behavior charts
- ☐ follow up rewards and consequences
- ☐ _____
- ☐ _____

Clerical Duties

- ☐ routine office duties (e.g., filing, typing, photocopying, answering the phone)
- ☐ maintain the database
- ☐ update teacher and student schedules
- ☐ _____
- ☐ _____

Data Collection

- ☐ collect and chart data obtained over specific periods
- ☐ document student progress
- ☐ transfer and record classroom data
- ☐ _____
- ☐ _____

Develop Materials (under the direction of a supervising professional)

- ☐ create individualized learning materials
- ☐ modify existing curriculum materials
- ☐ record materials on audiocassettes
- ☐ _____
- ☐ _____

Health-Related Services

- ☐ assist with lifting and rotating
- ☐ assist with personal hygiene, including feeding and diapering
- ☐ assist with motor or mobility limitations
- ☐ use specific medical equipment
- ☐ _____
- ☐ _____

(Continued)

Form 3, page 2

Organization Skills

- ☐ help students organize desks and lockers
- ☐ at the beginning of the day, help students unpack book bags and turn in homework
- ☐ at the end of the day, help students pack homework and the correct textbooks
- ☐ monitor specific students for organization skills
- ☐ _____
- ☐ _____

Reinforcement of Skills

- ☐ provide remedial instruction
- ☐ reteach previously taught skills
- ☐ play educational games
- ☐ _____
- ☐ _____

Supervision

- ☐ oversee small groups of students in the classroom
- ☐ monitor work completion
- ☐ supervise students during lunch, recess, and getting on and off the bus
- ☐ monitor students in common areas such as the hallways
- ☐ _____
- ☐ _____

Team Participation

- ☐ communicate with parents regarding homework or daily activities
- ☐ communicate with general education and special education teachers
- ☐ attend student conferences and IEP meetings
- ☐ attend all required meetings
- ☐ _____
- ☐ _____

Work With Students (large- and small-group or individual)

- ☐ help students with activities
- ☐ help students with make-up work
- ☐ help students with interpreting and following directions
- ☐ administer individual tests
- ☐ monitor and assist students during seatwork activities
- ☐ support students with daily assignments (in all areas)
- ☐ read aloud to students or provide support for independent reading
- ☐ _____
- ☐ _____
- ☐ _____
- ☐ _____

Form 4

General Responsibilities

Paraprofessional Responsibility	Training Needed	Follow-Up Date

Form 5

Roles and Responsibilities

Supervising Teacher	Paraprofessional

Form 6

Daily Schedule

Time	Location	Activity	Supervising Teacher

Form 7

Special Education Acronyms

ACB:	American Council for the Blind
ADA:	Americans with Disabilities Act
ADD:	attention deficit disorder
ADHD:	attention deficit hyperactivity disorder
APE:	adaptive physical education
ASL:	American Sign Language
AT:	assistive technology
BD:	behavior disorder
BIP:	behavior intervention plan
CA:	chronological age
CAPD:	central auditory processing disorder
CST:	child study team
DD:	developmental disability
DP:	due process
DVR:	Department of Vocational Rehabilitation
EBD:	emotional/behavioral disorder
EH:	emotionally handicapped
EMH:	educable mentally handicapped
ESL:	English as a second language
FAPE:	free and appropriate public education
FBA:	functional behavioral assessment
FERPA:	Family Education Rights and Privacy Act
GT:	gifted and talented
HI:	hearing impaired
IDEA:	Individuals with Disabilities Education Act

IDEIA:	Individuals with Disabilities Education Improvement Act
IEP:	individualized education plan
IFSP:	individualized family service plan
IQ:	intelligence quotient
LD:	learning disabilities
LEP:	limited English proficiency
LRE:	least restrictive environment
MR:	mental retardation
NRCP:	National Resource Center for Paraprofessionals in Education and Related Services
NVLD:	nonverbal learning disability
OHI:	other health impairment
OSEP:	Office of Special Education Programs
OT:	occupational therapy or occupational therapist
PDD:	Pervasive Developmental Disorder
PT:	physical therapy
SED:	serious (severe) emotional disturbance (disorder)
SI:	speech impairment or sensory integration
SLD:	specific learning (or language) disability
SLI:	speech and language impaired
SLP:	speech and language pathologist
SPED:	special education
TBI:	traumatic brain injury
VI:	visually impaired

Form 8

Daily Log

Student: _____	Date: _____	M T W TH F

Student: _____	Date: _____	M T W TH F

Student: _____	Date: _____	M T W TH F

Student: _____	Date: _____	M T W TH F

Form 9

Daily Communication

Student's Name: _____ Date: _____

Daily notes or comments:

❑   See me regarding this
❑   Speak to the classroom teacher
❑   Call the parent
❑   _____

- -

Student's Name: _____ Date: _____

Daily notes or comments:

❑   See me regarding this
❑   Speak to the classroom teacher
❑   Call the parent
❑   _____

- -

Student's Name: _____ Date: _____

Daily notes or comments:

❑   See me regarding this
❑   Speak to the classroom teacher
❑   Call the parent
❑   _____

Form 10

Alternate Plan

Student's Name: _____ Date: _____

Special Education Contact: _____

General Education Contact: _____

Backup Discipline Plan:

_____

_____

_____

_____

Additional Information:

_____

_____

_____

_____

_____

If assistance is needed, please call the following person(s):

Contact Person With Telephone Number

❏ Administrator   _____

❏ General Education   _____

❏ Special Education   _____

❏ Paraprofessional   _____

❏ Parent   _____

❏ _____   _____

❏ _____   _____

❏ _____   _____

Form 11

Medical Alert Form

Student's Name: _____

Special Education Contact: _____

General Education Contact: _____

❑ **This is an emergency. Call 911 immediately and then contact the following people.**

Contact Person and Telephone Number

1. _____

2. _____

3. _____

Notes: _____
_____
_____
_____

Area of Concern: _____
_____
_____
_____

Symptoms: _____
_____
_____
_____

Additional Information: _____
_____
_____
_____
_____

Copies:

❑ General Education   ❑ _____

❑ Special Education   ❑ _____

❑ Nurse   ❑ _____

❑ Paraprofessional   ❑ _____

❑ Parent

Form 12, page 1

Classroom Information

Classroom Teacher: _____   Subject or Grade: _____

Student(s):

_____

_____

_____

Classroom Schedule: (What is my daily schedule? When will student contact occur? Planning time?)

Classroom Instruction: (How will I help students in the classroom? Where and when will I receive training? What are your [the classroom teacher's] expectations? Will I be involved with student planning?)

(Continued)

Form 12, page 2

Classroom Information

Student Evaluation: (Will I have a role in student evaluation? Will I be expected to document and monitor student progress? If yes, who will provide training and guidance?)

Classroom Rules: (What are the classroom rules? Are all students expected to follow the same rules, or are there exceptions?)

Consequences: (Who is responsible for implementing the consequences if a student does not follow the rules? Are the consequences the same for all students? Are there rewards as well as consequences?)

Communication: (When will we find time to communicate our needs? Will I be expected to communicate with parents? When will we find time to communicate as a team? Who is my primary contact person?)

Use the back of this form to list additional information that is relevant to this classroom.

Form 13

Goal Worksheet

Student:_____ Subject Area: _____

General Education Teacher:_____

Special Education Teacher: _____

Date:
Final Goal:
Short-Term Objectives:

Date:
Final Goal:
Short-Term Objectives:

Date:
Final Goal:
Short-Term Objectives:

Form 14

Instructional Changes

Date: _____

Student: _____

Subject Area: _____

Area of Difficulty	Change Implemented	Result

Form 15, page 1

Curriculum

Date: _____

Student's Name: _____

Team Members: _____

_____

_____

_____

List the student's strengths:

List the student's goals:

MODIFICATIONS
Textbook: Person responsible for follow-up:
Daily Assignments: Person responsible for follow-up:
Spelling: Person responsible for follow-up:

(Continued)

Form 15, page 2

Curriculum

Mathematics: Person responsible for follow-up:
Organizational Skills: Person responsible for follow-up:
Directions: Person responsible for follow-up:
Large-Group Instruction: Person responsible for follow-up:
Assessment: Person responsible for follow-up:
Behavior: Person responsible for follow-up:
Additional Areas of Concern: (Use the back side of this form if more space is needed.)

Form 16, page 1

Textbooks

Student's Name: _____ Date: _____

Subject Area: _____ Grade level: _____

Team Members:

Check all that apply:

❑ The student will need modifications to the classroom textbook.
❑ The student should read the textbook with a peer or in a small group.
❑ The textbook should be provided on audiocassette.
   ❑ Full-text version
   ❑ Paraphrase
   ❑ Alternate format _____

❑ Other: _____
❑ Other: _____
❑ Other: _____

Name of person responsible: _____

Check all that apply:

❑ The student will need the following supplemental services: _____
   ❑ Preteaching and previewing of the material
   ❑ Outline of required units
   ❑ List of vocabulary words
   ❑ Checklist of required assignments and due dates
   ❑ Study guide
   ❑ Set of textbooks for home use

❑ Other: _____
❑ Other: _____
❑ Other: _____

Name of person responsible: _____

(Continued)

Form 16, page 2

Textbooks

Check all that apply:

❑ The student will require direct support from the Special Education Department.
❑ Supplemental curriculum is needed.
    ❑ Other: _____
    ❑ Other: _____
    ❑ Other: _____
    ❑ Other: _____

Direct instruction to be provided by: _____

Location of direct service: _____

Time of day: _____

❑ Support needed in the classroom
    ❑ Other: _____
    ❑ Other: _____
    ❑ Other: _____
    ❑ Other: _____

Name of person responsible: _____

Additional information:

Form 17, page 1

Daily Assignments

Student's Name: _____ Date: _____

Subject Area: _____ Grade Level: _____

Team Members:

Check all that apply:

❏ The student will need the following applied to daily assignments:
  ❏ Modify the length of the assignment.
  ❏ Place the student in cooperative groups whenever possible.
  ❏ Allow the student to complete assignments orally.
  ❏ Allow material to be read to the student.
  ❏ Allow assignments to be written for the student.
  ❏ Give the student extra time to complete assignments.
  ❏ The student is required to keep an assignment book.
  ❏ Other: _____
  ❏ Other: _____
  ❏ Other: _____
  ❏ Other: _____
  ❏ Other: _____

Name of person responsible: _____

Check all that apply:

❏ The student will need the following supplemental material and services:
  ❏ A checklist of assignments and due dates
  ❏ Textbooks for home use
  ❏ Consumable textbooks
  ❏ Other: _____
  ❏ Other: _____
  ❏ Other: _____
  ❏ Other: _____
  ❏ Other: _____

Name of person responsible: _____

(Continued)

Form 17, page 2

Daily Assignments

Check all that apply:

❏ The student will require direct support from the Special Education Department.

Amount of service provided daily: _____

Location and time of service: _____

Name of person responsible: _____

❏ Supplemental curriculum will be provided.

Alternative curriculum will be provided by _____

Parallel activities will be provided by_____

  ❏ Other: _____
  ❏ Other: _____
  ❏ Other: _____

Name of person responsible: _____

Additional information:

Form 18

Assessments

Student's Name: _____ Date: _____

Subject Area: _____ Grade Level: _____

Team Members:

Check all that apply:

❏ The student will need the following applied to assessment situations:
    ❏ Allow extra or extended time.
    ❏ Review materials with student prior to assessment.
    ❏ Read the test aloud.
    ❏ Student may respond to questions orally.
    ❏ Student may use a vocabulary list during assessment.
    ❏ Student may dictate or record the answers.
    ❏ Assessment questions may be reworded and explained.
    ❏ Student is allowed to use notes or a study guide during assessment.
    ❏ Student may use a calculator.
    ❏ Student may use a computer.
    ❏ Student may work with another student.
    ❏ Other: _____
    ❏ Other: _____
    ❏ Other: _____
    ❏ Other: _____
    ❏ Other: _____
    ❏ Other: _____

❏ Additional information:

❏ Person responsible for creating the modification: _____

Form 19

Volunteer List

Student Name	Dates				

Form 20

Daily Assignment Log

Date	Subject Area	Assignment	Due Date	Complete √

Form 21

Weekly Assignments

Subject Area	Monday	Tuesday	Wednesday	Thursday	Friday
Math					
Social Studies					
English					
Science					
Tests					
Projects					

Form 22

Common Abbreviations for Note Taking

2	to	hr	hour	tm	time
&	and	hsty	history	u	you
abv	above	ht	height	un	unit
aft	after	illus	illustration	v	very
amt	amount	imp	important	w	with
ans	answer	inc	incomplete	w/o	without
assn	association	info	information	wd	wide
b/c	because	lb	pound	wdth	width
bf	before	masc	masculine	whn	when
bgn	begin	med	medium	wht	what
bib	bibliography	min	minute	yr	year
biog	biography	mny	many	mth	month
blw	below	mph	miles per hour		
cap	capital	mth	month		
comp	complete	n/t	next to		
dept	department	no	number		
dur	during	nt	not		
ea	each	opp	opposite		
ed	edition	pop	population		
etc	et cetera	pp	pages		
ex	example	ppl	people		
exer	exercise	prob	problem		
F	Fahrenheit	sec	section		
fin	finish	sec	second		
freq	frequency	sq	square		
gd	good	t/o	throughout		
govt	government	thru	through		

Add your own abbreviations to the list.

Form 23

Chapter Outline

1. _____

    a. _____

    b. _____

    c. _____

2. _____

    a. _____

    b. _____

    c. _____

3. _____

    a. _____

    b. _____

    c. _____

Form 24

Compare and Contrast

Attribute	#1	#2

Form 25

Weekly Study Schedule

Time	Monday	Tuesday	Wednesday	Thursday	Friday
3:00–3:30					
3:30–4:00					
4:00–4:30					
4:30–5:00					
5:00–5:30					
5:30–6:00					
6:00–6:30					
6:30–7:00					
7:00–7:30					
7:30–8:00					
8:00–8:30					
8:30–9:00					
9:00–9:30					
9:30–10:00					

Block out the following time blocks on the schedule:
study time, afterschool activities, athletics, dinner, and free time.

Form 26

Priority Assignment Sheet

Date	Priority Rating	Assignment	Time Allotment	Date Completed

Use a pencil to fill in the information. The priority list will change as the assignments are completed.

Date: Write in the date that the assignment was given.

Priority Rating: Prioritize the assignment. The assignment listed as #1 should receive the highest priority.

Assignment: List the assignment and subject area.

Time Allotment: Estimate the amount of time needed to complete the assignment.

Date Completed: When you complete the assignment, place a check in the box and list the date the assignment is complete.

Form 27

My To-Do List

1. _____

2. _____

3. _____

4. _____

5. _____

6. _____

Reminders!

1. _____

2. _____

3. _____

4 _____

Form 28

Checklist: Materials to Take Home

	Monday	Tuesday	Wednesday	Thursday	Friday
Assignment Book:	_____	_____	_____	_____	_____
Textbooks:					
English	_____	_____	_____	_____	_____
Math	_____	_____	_____	_____	_____
Social Studies	_____	_____	_____	_____	_____
English	_____	_____	_____	_____	_____
Science	_____	_____	_____	_____	_____
_____	_____	_____	_____	_____	_____
_____	_____	_____	_____	_____	_____
Supplies:					
Pencils/pens	_____	_____	_____	_____	_____
Colored pencils	_____	_____	_____	_____	_____
Markers	_____	_____	_____	_____	_____
Calculator	_____	_____	_____	_____	_____
_____	_____	_____	_____	_____	_____
_____	_____	_____	_____	_____	_____
Handouts:					
_____	_____	_____	_____	_____	_____
_____	_____	_____	_____	_____	_____
_____	_____	_____	_____	_____	_____
Study Guides:					
_____	_____	_____	_____	_____	_____
_____	_____	_____	_____	_____	_____
_____	_____	_____	_____	_____	_____
Graded Tests:					
_____	_____	_____	_____	_____	_____
_____	_____	_____	_____	_____	_____
_____	_____	_____	_____	_____	_____
Materials for Parent:					
_____	_____	_____	_____	_____	_____
_____	_____	_____	_____	_____	_____

Form 29, page 1

Alphabet Activities

Letter	Activity
A	**Apple Art**. Cut an apple in half so that you can see the star. Students dip the apple in paint and make apple prints. *A* **Words on Apples**. Students cut out various colored apples from construction paper, place *a* words on the apples, and create an apple tree.
B	**Bean Art**. Give students several different kinds of dried beans so that they can glue the beans to construction paper to make a design. **Bag of** *B* **Words**. Give each student a small brown bag. Ask them to fill the bags with pictures of *b* words.
C	**Collage Art**. Help students find pictures of things that begin with *c* in old magazines, or select a subject such as cats, candy, or colors. Students then make a collage with the pictures. **Can of** *C* **Words**. Students fill a Campbell's soup can with words beginning with *c*.
D	**Magic Door Art**. Cut four to six doors in a piece of colored construction paper. Glue the construction paper on top of another piece of construction paper or tag board. Students draw pictures of *d* words behind each door. **Magic Door Story**. Students write a simple story about the items found behind the magic door.
E	**Egg Art**. Punch a small hole in one end of an egg and a larger hole in the other end. Blow out the contents and rinse the egg. Students can decorate the egg with markers or paints. **Envelope of** *E* **Words**. Students fill an envelope with *e* words.
F	**Fishbowl Art**. Students cut small fish shapes out of construction paper and write *f* words on them. Then they decorate the fish and glue them into a large fish bowl. **Fire Prevention Discussion**. Discuss fire prevention and fire drills with students.
G	**Garden Art**. Students draw a garden with various flowers. The flowers may be decorated with glue and glitter. **Grocery Graph**. Create a grocery graph. Students cut out pictures from grocery ads and classify the items into groups on a large piece of construction paper.

Form 29, page 2

Alphabet Activities

H	**Body Parts**. Trace each student's body on a large sheet of paper. Label the body parts that begin with *h*: hair, hands, heart, heel, head, and hips.
	Happy List. What makes me happy? Students create a list of happy thoughts.
I	**Insect Art**. Students draw pictures of insects. Remember that insects have six legs, and their bodies are made up of the head, thorax, and abdomen. Label the body parts.
	I **Sentences**. Students practice writing *i* sentences.
J	**Jewelry Art**. Students string macaroni and make a piece of jewelry.
	Jelly Bean Sort. Give each student a handful of jelly beans so that they can sort the jelly beans by color.
K	**Kangaroo Art**. Provide a kite template for students to cut out and decorate. They can add colored ribbon or string. Students draw pictures of *k* words and decorate the kites.
	Random Acts of Kindness. Discuss kindness with students, and ask each student to do some secret kind acts for friends and family.
L	**Leaf Art**. Provide an assortment of leaves and crayons or chalk. Students make leaf rubbings on paper.
	Lazy Discussion. Talk with students about what it means to be lazy. Students then write a group story about a lazy animal such as a lion, ladybug, lizard, or lamb.
M	**Macaroni or Mini Marshmallow Art**. Provide various shapes of macaroni or colored mini marshmallows. Students decorate a large *m* by gluing the macaroni and marshmallows to the letter.
	Map Creation. Look around the room and discuss the various maps. Ask students to make a map of their classroom.
N	**Nutrition Art**. Provide students with paper plates. They cut out pictures of various healthy foods and glue the pictures to their plates to create a nutritious meal.
	Nurse Visit. Visit the school nurse, and have students ask questions about the nurse's job.

(Continued)

Form 29, page 3

Alphabet Activities

O	**Opposite Art**. Discuss the concept of opposites, and have students make a small book depicting such opposites as day/night, white/black, up/down, open/close, happy/sad, and over/under. **Occupation Discussion**. Discuss the word *occupation*, and talk about what students would like to do as adults.
P	**Pipe Cleaner Art**. Provide students with several different-colored pipe cleaners, and have them make sculptures. **Pocket Game**. Take turns placing small objects in your pocket. Begin by saying "I have something in my pocket . . ." and describe the item. Have students guess what you are hiding.
Q	**Q-tip Art**. Give each student three or four Q-tips. Students can dip them in paint and create a picture. **Quiet Discussion**. Discuss the word *quiet*. What does mean? When is it important to be quiet and why?
R	**Rock Art**. Students paint rocks to use as paperweights. **Recycling Discussion**. Discuss the importance of recycling. Have students label paper bags and sort the various papers (plain, glossy, newsprint) for recycling.
S	**Sponge-Painting Art**. Cut a large sponge into small squares. Students dip sponges into paint and create designs on white construction paper. **Share Discussion**. Discuss the word *share*. Student may bring something from home to share.
T	**Tear Art**. Students tear small pieces of leftover paper and glue them together to make a picture or a design. **Taste and Touch Discussion**. Discuss the five senses, emphasizing taste and touch. For taste, bring samples of various spices from home for the student to taste (a small pinch of sugar, salt, cinnamon, etc.). For touch, enclose small objects in paper bags, and ask students to guess what each object is without looking.

Form 29, page 4

Alphabet Activities

U	**Undersea Art**. Using crayons on white construction paper, students draw pictures of undersea animals. When finished, they use blue tempera paint diluted with water to paint over the entire picture. **Under/Upside-Down Discussion**. Discuss the words *under* and *upside-down*. Students list as many objects as possible in the classrooms that are under something. Determine the effect when some objects are upside down. For example, what would happen if the wastebasket or an open jar of paint were turned upside down?
V	**Vacation Art**. Students draw pictures of a previous vacation or a dream vacation to share. **Vacation Discussion**. Discuss types of vacations and various transportation options: car, airplane, boat, and train.
W	**Web Art**. Students use white chalk and black paper to draw interesting spider web designs. They create small white spiders to dangle from their webs on white string. **Weigh-In**. Walk to the nurse's office, and weigh each student. If there is a science scale in the classroom, students can practice weighing various classroom objects.
X	**Cross-Stitch Art**. Students use graph paper to make designs filled in by Xs. **X-ray Discussion**. Discuss the use of X-rays (broken bones, airport screening, etc.). Find pictures of X-ray results to share with students.
Y	**Yarn Art**. Provide students with yellow yarn in various lengths. Students place thin lines of glue on a piece of yellow construction paper and secure the yarn to the glue. Students may also use yellow glitter and fabric to complete their designs. **Yellow Light Discussion**. Discuss the reason for signal lights, emphasizing the "caution" (yellow) light.
Z	**Zoo Art**. Students create imaginary animals on white construction paper. They cut strips of colored paper and glue them onto the paper to make a cage. Have them give the animals *z* names. **Zip-top Bag of Z Words**. Give students zip-top bags and have them put *z* words into the bags.

Some of these ideas were adapted from Hands-On-Phonics for Elementary Children (Stangl, 2000), which is an excellent resource for beginning readers.

Form 30, page 1

Alphabet Cards

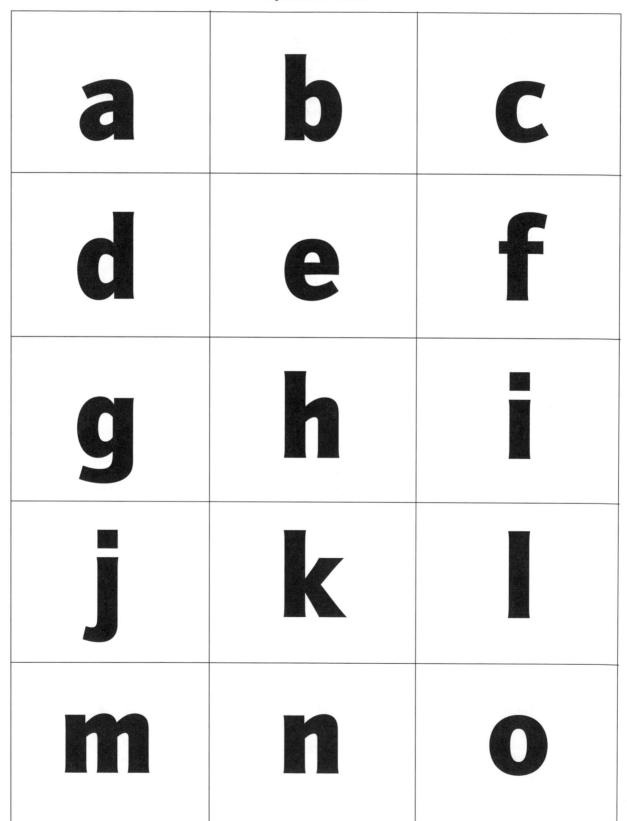

Form 30, page 2

p	q	r
s	t	u
v	w	x
y	z	
Sounds I Know!	Sounds to Practice!	

Form 31

Common Word Families

Beginning Word Families		More Advanced Word Families	
-am	am, ham, jam, Pam	**-all**	ball, hall, mall, tall
-an	an, can, fan, man	**-ame**	blame, came, fame, game
-ap	cap, gap, lap, map	**-ank**	bank, rank, sank, tank
-at	at, cat, fat, hat	**-ash**	cash, flash, rash, trash
-ay	day, gay, hay, say	**-ate**	date, fate, mate, plate
-ed	bed, fed, led, red	**-eat**	beat, feat, heat, treat
-ew	dew, few, new, pew	**-eed**	deed, feed, heed, seed
		-est	best, nest, pest, test
-in	fin, win, pin, chin		
-ip	dip, hip, lip, flip	**-ice**	dice, mice, nice, price
-it	it, bit, fit, sit	**-ick**	kick, lick, sick, brick
		-ide	hide, ride, pride, tide
-op	hop, mop, pop, crop	**-ight**	light, night, right, sight
-ot	dot, got, lot, plot	**-ill**	fill, hill, pill, will
-ow	bow, cow, how, now	**-ine**	fine, line, mine, vine
		-ink	link, pink, sink, wink
-ug	bug, dug, hug, rug		
-up	up, cup, pup	**-ock**	dock, lock, clock, shock
-um	gum, drum, hum, plum	**-oke**	joke, choke, croak, poke
		-out	pout, scout, shout, trout
-ack	lack, tack, black, sack		
-ade	fade, made, blade, shade	**-uck**	buck, puck, suck, stuck
-ail	bail, hail, nail, pail	**-ump**	bump, clump, dump, lump

Form 32, page 1

Basic Phonics Rules

Use these basic phonics rules to help students read and write better. The English language is very complex, so this list is very short and by no means all-inclusive.

Short Vowels

- A short vowel sound corresponds to the sound in the following sample words: *cat, pet, hit, hot, cut.*

- Closed-syllable rule: If a vowel is located in the middle of a one-syllable word (*hat, sun, not*), the vowel usually has a short sound.

- If there is one *e* in a word and the word ends with a consonant (*help, next, spell*), the *e* usually has the short sound.

- If a word ends in *ck*, the *k* sound is heard and the preceding vowel is short (*chick, pack, stock*).

Long Vowels

- If two vowels are together in a word (*coat, main, people, dream*), the first vowel is usually long and the second vowel is silent.

- If there is only one vowel at the end of a word, it is usually long (*be, so, me*).

- If a word has one vowel in the middle and ends with the letter *e* (*cake, side, close*), the middle vowel usually has a long sound and the final *e* is silent.

(Continued)

Form 32, page 2

Basic Phonics Rules

- Words with a double *e* (*seen, green*) usually take on the long *e* sound.

- If a word ends with *ay* (*day, play, say*), the *a* takes on a long sound and the *y* is silent.

- If *i* is followed by *gh* (*night, flight*), the *i* takes on the long sound and the *gh* is silent.

Additional Rules

- Modified Vowels: If the medial vowel is followed by an *r* (*cure, harm, firm*), it becomes an *r*-controlled vowel and usually has neither a long nor short sound.

- The *ie* combination (*thief, pie, field*) is frequently used, but this combination does not follow the consonant *c* (*receive*).

- The vowel combination *ea* may take either a long (*seat*) or short (*bread*) sound.

- When certain consonants are positioned together, they usually make one sound (*church, there, white, bomb, telephone, knight, back, write, gnat*).

- If *c* is followed by one of the vowels *a, o,* or *u*, the sound of *k* is usually heard. If *c* is followed by the vowels *e* or *i*, the sound of *s* is usually heard.

Form 33, page 1

Dolch Word List

Preprimer				
a	and	away	big	blue
can	come	down	find	for
funny	go	help	here	I
in	is	it	little	look
make	me	my	not	one
play	red	run	said	see
the	three	to	two	up
we	where	yellow	you	

Primer				
all	am	are	at	ate
be	black	brown	but	came
did	do	eat	four	get
good	have	he	into	like
must	new	no	now	on
our	out	please	pretty	ran
ride	saw	say	she	so
soon	that	there	they	this
too	under	want	was	well
went	what	white	who	will
with	yes			

(Continued)

Form 33, page 2

Level One				
after	again	an	any	as
ask	by	could	every	fly
from	give	going	had	has
her	him	his	how	jump
just	know	let	live	may
of	old	once	open	over
put	round	some	stop	take
thank	them	then	think	walk
warm	were	when		

Level Two				
always	around	because	been	before
best	both	buy	call	cold
does	don't	fast	first	five
found	gave	goes	green	its
made	many	off	or	pull
read	right	sing	sit	sleep
tell	their	these	those	upon
us	use	very	wash	which
why	wish	work	would	write
your				

Form 33, page 3

Level Three				
about	better	bring	carry	clean
cut	done	draw	drink	eight
fall	far	full	got	grow
hold	hot	hurt	if	keep
kind	laugh	light	long	much
myself	never	only	own	pick
seven	shall	show	six	small
start	ten	today	together	try

Form 34

Instant Words

This list of 100 words makes up almost one-half of all written material.

Words 1–25	Words 26–50	Words 51–75	Words 75–100
the	or	will	number
of	one	up	no
and	had	other	way
a	by	about	could
to	word	out	people
in	but	many	my
is	not	then	than
you	what	them	first
that	all	these	water
it	were	so	been
he	we	some	call
was	when	her	who
for	your	would	oil
on	can	make	its
are	said	like	now
as	there	him	find
with	use	into	long
his	an	time	down
they	each	has	day
I	which	look	did
at	she	two	get
be	do	more	come
this	how	write	made
have	their	go	may
from	if	see	part

Form 35

Bingo Game Grid

B	I	N	G	O

Form 36

Tic-Tac-Toe Grid

Create cards to reinforce letter sounds, word families, sight words, vocabulary words, and definitions. The student needs to read the card, or answer the question, in order to place a chip on the Tic-Tac-Toe Grid.

Form 37

Word List

Word I Read	Correct Word

Form 38

Story Organizer

Title:	

Main Character:	Character #2:
Character #3:	Character #4:

Where does the story take place?

What is the first major event of the story?

Is there an additional important event?

Is there a problem that needs to be solved?

Is there additional important information that should be listed?

How does the story end?

Form 39

Common Prefixes and Suffixes

Prefix	Meaning	Sample Words
anti-	against	antiwar, antislavery
be-	make	befriend
bi-	two	bicycle, bifocals
circu-	around	circulate, circumference
contra-	against, opposite	contrary, contrast
dis-	not	disagree, disappear
ex-	former	ex-president, ex-student
hyper-	excessive	hyperactive, hypersensitive
in-	into	inside, infiltrate
inter-	among, between	intermission, interrupt
intra-	within	intravenous, intramural
mid-	middle	midway, midyear
mis-	wrong, not	mistake, misunderstand
multi-	many, much	multiply, multicolored
non-	not	nonfiction, nonstop
para-	almost	paramedic, paralegal
post-	after	postdate, postwar
pre-	before	pretest, prefix
pro-	favor	pro-war, pro-education
re-	again	remake, reread
sub-	under	subway, subzero
tele-	distant	telephone, telescope
tri-	three	tricycle, tripod
un-	not	unable, unhappy
uni-	one	unicorn, unison

Suffix	Meaning	Sample Words
-able, -ible	is, can be	climbable, gullible
-an	relating to	veteran, American
-ar, -er, -or	one, who	liar, teacher, editor
-er	more	smarter, luckier
-en	to make	fasten, weaken
-ess	one who (female)	waitress, actress
-est	most	closest, lightest
-ful	full of	joyful, fearful
-ish	relating to	bookish, selfish
-less	without	tireless, careless
-like	resembling	childlike, lifelike
-ly	resembling	motherly, sisterly
-ment	action, process	development, experiment
-ness	quality of	kindness, darkness

Form 40

Charting New Vocabulary

Vocabulary Word:	
What does the word mean?	What is an antonym for this word?
Use the word in a sentence.	Use the antonym in a sentence.
List additional synonyms for this word.	

Vocabulary Word:	
What does the word mean?	What is an antonym for this word?
Use the word in a sentence.	Use the antonym in a sentence.
List additional synonyms for this word.	

Form 41, page 1

Story Starters

Titles

The Day I Missed My Own Party	The Mysterious Key
The African Safari	I Really Saw an Alien!
The Day I Made the News	The Day the Sun Did Not Set
The Time Machine	9-1-1
The Grand Slam	Lost in the Forest (or Jungle, Cave, etc.)
The Tornado (or Hurricane, Earthquake, etc.)	The Substitute Teacher
The Fire	My Secret Powers
Help! I'm Invisible! (or Shrinking, Growing, etc.)	If I Were an Octopus (or Barracuda, Shark, etc.)
If I Were the Principal (or President, Teacher, etc.)	A Horrible (or Wonderful, Depressing, etc.) Day
The Rescue	HELP!
If My Dog (or Cat, Horse, etc.) Could Talk	The Best Vacation Ever!

Beginning Sentences

I was sinking deeper and deeper into the quicksand . . . .

I heard a loud growl directly behind me . . . .

As the airplane reached full altitude, I sat back and closed my eyes. Finally . . . .

I must have been dreaming. I sat up and looked around. Everything was different . . . .

Susan heard a scream. She ran to the lake to find her little brother . . . .

I looked at the small snake in the box. My parents will never find out . . . .

I slammed on the brakes. "Please stop!" I prayed . . . .

(Continued)

Form 41, page 2

Story Starters

Beginning Sentences (continued)

I tried to run, but the wind was so strong . . . .

I hit the snooze button on the alarm for the third time. I just cannot go to school today . . . .

I heard the rustle of the leaves. Slowly I walked toward the sound. Imagine my surprise when I found . . . .

I picked up the wallet from the ground and opened it. The wallet had over $1,000 in cash . . . .

Unbelievable Excuses

I don't have my homework because . . . .

I ate the entire gallon of ice cream because . . . .

I had to have my cell phone in class because . . . .

I missed volleyball practice because . . . .

I couldn't clean my bedroom because . . . .

I didn't study for the test because . . . .

I pretended to be sick because . . . .

I gave the dog a haircut because . . . .

I crawled out the window at 2:00 a.m. because . . . .

I was late because . . . .

I didn't go to school because . . . .

I lied because . . . .

I put worms in the sink because . . . .

I had to skip class because . . . .

I had to go to the movie because . . . .

I dyed my hair green because . . . .

I had to skip class because . . . .

I missed the bus because . . . .

Form 42, page 1

Story Planner

Title: _____

Setting: _____

Season: _____

Time of Day: _____

Main Characters (include description also):

Character #1: _____

_____

_____

_____

Character #2: _____

_____

_____

_____

Character #3: _____

_____

_____

_____

_____

_____

(Continued)

Form 42, page 2

Story Planner

How does the story begin? _____

_____

List at least one major event which occurs in the story:

Event #1: _____

_____

Event #2: _____

_____

Event #3: _____

_____

How does the story end? _____

_____

_____

_____

Form 43

Story Outline

1. Who is the main character in the story?

_____

_____

_____

2. List the other characters in the story: _____

_____

_____

_____

3. What does the main character want to do (accomplish, solve) in the story?

_____

_____

_____

4. List the main events in the order in which they occur:

Event #1: _____

_____

_____

Event #2: _____

_____

_____

Event #3: _____

_____

_____

5. What happens as a result of the action or event? _____

_____

_____

6. How does the story end? _____

_____

_____

7. Use the back of the page to list any additional information you would like to include.

Form 44

Proofreading Checklist

Capital letters	☐ beginning of sentences ☐ names ☐ specific places ☐ title of story
Punctuation	☐ . ☐ ? ☐ !
Spelling	☐ dictionary ☐ notes

☐ Spelling ☐ Punctuation ☐ Capital Letters ☐ Paragraphs 　☐ Indentation 　☐ Topic sentence 　☐ Details ☐ Margins ☐ Overall appearance ☐ Name, date, class period	☐ **Spelling** ☐ **Punctuation** ☐ **Appearance** ☐ **Capitalization** ☐ **Error analysis**

Form 45, page 1

Paragraph Sequencing Activity

Each paragraph below contains mixed-up sentences. Read the sentences carefully. When you finish, cut the sentences apart and put them in the correct order so the paragraph makes sense.

Sample Paragraph

Mary then gathered the supplies needed to mix the cake.

She took the box of cake mix out of the cupboard and read the directions.

Thirty minutes later the timer went off and the cake was finished.

Once the batter was mixed, she poured it into the pan and put the pan in the oven.

Mary decided to bake a cake for her mother's birthday.

Sample Paragraph

He knew he had to clean it, but did not know where to begin.

Once it was picked up and put away, John decided to vacuum.

John's bedroom was a mess.

He decided first to pick up all the stuff on the floor.

After several hours, the job was finally complete.

(Continued)

Form 45, page 2

Paragraph Sequencing Activity
Sample Paragraph

Alisa knew she had to hurry or she would miss the school bus.

She grabbed her coat and mittens from the front closet.

She quickly put on her coat and zipped it up.

Next she put on her mittens.

She grabbed her backpack and rushed out the door to catch the bus.

Sample Paragraph

As he was mentally preparing to jump into the pool, the fire alarm sounded.

"I really don't feel like swimming 50 laps today," he thought as he entered the pool area.

"Yes! Saved by the alarm," he shouted as he grabbed his warm-ups and headed for the exit.

He then walked over to the pool to test the water.

It felt cold as ice, and John shivered at the thought of jumping in.

He removed his warm-ups and threw them onto the bench.

John was in a terrible mood as he left the men's locker room.

Form 45, page 3

Paragraph Sequencing Activity

Name: _____

Date: _____

_____

(Title)

Form 46

Study Methods for Spelling

Read-and-Spell Method

☐ Look at the word while it is read aloud.

☐ Read the word aloud. Spell the word aloud. Read the word again.

☐ Spell the word two times without looking at the model.

☐ Compare the word to the model.

Hear-and-Spell Method

☐ Observe while the word is written on a flash card, the board, or the overhead projector.

☐ Read the word aloud. Listen while each letter is read aloud to you.

☐ Listen while each letter of the word is read aloud, and repeat each letter.

☐ Spell the word aloud alone.

Cover-and-Write Method

☐ Read the word aloud from the model.

☐ Turn the model over (or cover it), and spell the word without looking.

☐ While viewing the word, write it on a piece of paper.

☐ Compare the word to the model.

☐ If the word is correct, write it three more times without looking at the model.

☐ Compare your word to the model. If it is correct, select another word to practice.

Form 47

"What Do I Do if . . . ?"

These questions may be used as discussion points with the supervising teacher. You may also want to record some of the ideas from that discussion here.

. . . a student refuses to do the required assignment?

. . . a student is asked to begin the work and refuses?

. . . a student rips up the assignment?

. . . a student continually blurts out answers during small-group instruction?

. . . I ask a student to leave a small group and the student refuses?

. . . a student is instructed to clean up a mess that he or she has created and refuses?

. . . a student talks back or responds in an inappropriate manner?

. . . a student gets angry and starts throwing objects in the classroom?

. . . a student runs in the hall, classroom, etc., and, after being asked to stop, refuses to do so?

. . . a students runs away from me?

. . . a student continually swears quietly at his or her desk?

. . . a student hits and/or personally assaults another student?

. . . a student has an outburst in the classroom, which disrupts the entire class?

. . . a student starts to yell profanity to both adults and the other students?

. . . a student hits, pokes, and bothers other students in the classroom?

. . . a student continually arrives late to class?

. . . a student leaves the classroom without permission?

. . . a student leaves the classroom and does not return in the expected time frame?

Form 48

Behavior Change Plan

What happened? (list the incident that occurred)	What happened before the incident? (list the activity, subject, or any helpful information)	How did I respond?	What are some alternate responses if this situation reoccurs?

Additional support needed or comments:

Form 49

Tally Sheet

Student	Date/Time	Observable Behavior
	Tally Space	
		Total
		Total
		Total
		Total

Tally Sheet

Student	Date/Time	Observable Behavior
	Tally Space	
		Total
		Total
		Total
		Total

Form 50, page 1

Sample Reinforcement Charts

These charts may be reproduced and used for multiple purposes. For this reason, headers have not been included on the charts.

Sample 1. This chart may be used for homework assignments, work completion, behavior, and so on.

Subject/Date	**Monday**	**Tuesday**	**Wednesday**	**Thursday**	**Friday**

Sample 2. This chart may be used for behaviors that need to be documented frequently throughout the day.

Form 50, page 2

Sample Reinforcement Charts

For younger children, picture charts may be motivating. The following outlines may be used in several ways:

- Simple pictures may be cut apart into puzzle pieces. The student receives one puzzle piece as reinforcement. When the puzzle is complete, the student takes it home or turns it in for a reward.

- Simple dot-to-dot pictures may be created. For example, the points of a star could be numbered 1–10. The student connects the numbers, and when the dot-to-dot is complete, the student receives a reward.

(Continued)

Form 50, page 3

Sample Reinforcement Charts

The following charts may be used for students who require frequent feedback. List the target goal; at each check period, the student inserts a + or − in each box. The * indicates a reinforcement or reward if the goal has been met. In the first sample, the reinforcement would occur after two documented pluses. The following samples may be individualized for the student.

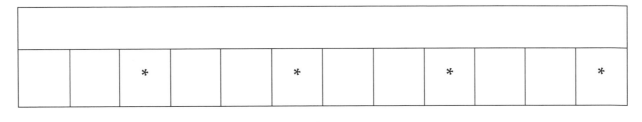

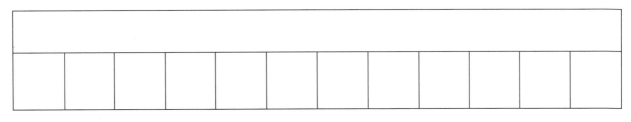

Form 50, page 4

Sample Reinforcement Charts

The following is a ladder chart. The student may color in the blocks and turn it in when the entire ladder is filled. In the sample, rewards have been included randomly on the chart.

Sample

	Step 8 You have reached your goal.
	Step 7
	Step 6 Select a reward!
	Step 5
	Step 4
	Step 3 Five minutes of free time
	Step 2
	Step 1

	Step 8
	Step 7
	Step 6
	Step 5
	Step 4
	Step 3
	Step 2
	Step 1

Photocopy the following onto sheets of self-adhesive label paper. The student may cut them apart and stick the symbols onto the chart.

♥	♥	♥	♥	♥	♥	♥	♥	♥	♥	♥	♥
♣	♣	♣	♣	♣	♣	♣	♣	♣	♣	♣	♣
☺	☺	☺	☺	☺	☺	☺	☺	☺	☺	☺	☺
+	+	+	+	+	+	+	+	+	+	+	+

Form 51, page 1

Positive Reinforcement Phrases

Awesome!

Wow!

I discovered the secret to success!

Fantastic day!

Way to go!

Form 51, page 2

Positive Reinforcement Phrases

Superstar!

Congratulations!

I'm on a roll!

I had a great day today!

I am special!

Form 52

Point Sheet

Subject	Teacher	Number of Points Earned	Homework/Comment Section

Criteria

3 points _____

2 points _____

1 points _____

0 points _____

Glossary

abstract thinking—ability to think in terms of ideas.

accommodation—supports provided throughout the school day that do not significantly alter what is being taught or how the student participates in school activities. Examples include preferential seating, extended time on test, use of a spell-checker, enlarged print, and books on tape.

adaptation—change that is made to the curriculum, instruction, environment, or material for an individual student.

ADD—see attention deficit disorder.

alternate assessments—an evaluation using various methods in place of traditional paper/pencil tests to assess a student's knowledge. Demonstrations, oral presentations, or projects are some examples.

attention deficit disorder—a condition in which a student has difficulties directing or maintaining attention to normal tasks involved in learning.

auditory blending—blending of sounds into words.

auditory discrimination—ability to hear differences and similarities in spoken words.

auditory memory—ability to recall information that is heard.

behavior—a relationship between a stimulus and a response.

behavior modification—process that creates a change in the stimulus–response pattern.

cognitive ability—the ability to learn. Cognitive ability testing may also be referred to as intelligence testing.

collaboration—to work together toward a common goal.

configuration cues—the outline of a word in relation to its shape and length.

confidentiality—the limiting of access to a student's or family's records to personnel having direct involvement with the student.

contract—a written agreement between teacher and student that outlines specific behaviors and consequences.

cumulative file—a file containing report cards, standardized achievement test scores, teacher reports, and other records of a student's school program.

curricular modifications—changes to the actual curriculum. Curricular modifications are created by certified teaching staff.

disability—a problem or condition that makes it hard for a student to learn or do things in the same ways as most other students. A disability may be short-term or permanent.

discrimination—ability to differentiate between visual, auditory, tactual, or other sensory stimuli.

distractibility—attention that is easily drawn away from the task.

due process—a system of procedures ensuring that an individual will be notified of and have the opportunity to contest decisions. Pertaining to special education, due process refers to the legal rights to appeal a decision regarding any portion of the process (evaluation, eligibility, individualized education plan, or placement).

eligibility—the determination of whether a child qualifies to receive services based on established criteria.

expressive language—the ability to communicate through speech, gestures, augmentative devices, or in writing.

fine motor skills—body movements that use small muscle groups for specific tasks such as handwriting, cutting, pasting, and eating.

gross motor skills—body movements that use large muscles for tasks such as sitting, walking, and climbing.

hyperactivity—excessive activity in relation to others of the same age and in similar situations.

IEP—See individualized education plan.

inclusive education—providing necessary supports and services so that children with disabilities can participate with children who do not have disabilities in school, community, and recreation activities.

individualized education plan—a written plan designed for an individual student who receives special education services. It describes the student's present level of performance, annual goals, specific special education and related services, dates for beginning and duration of services, and how the plan will be evaluated.

impulsivity—acting or speaking out without considering the consequences.

inclusion paraprofessional—a person who works with a specific group of students in an inclusive classroom.

inclusive education pupil paraprofessional—a person who is assigned to support a specific student. The assistant is written into the individualized education plan.

inclusive schooling—a school setting in which students receive educational instruction within the classroom setting for the entire or a substantial portion of the school day.

least restrictive environment—a setting that allows a student with disabilities to have maximum contact with students who do not have disabilities, while appropriately meeting the student's special education needs.

modifications—changes made to instruction or the curriculum that fundamentally change what the student is expected to learn. Examples of modifications include providing instruction to the student at a different academic level and testing different knowledge or skills than other students in the classroom.

memory—recall of visual, auditory, and/or tactile stimuli.

mnemonics—visual or word-related aids that facilitate retrieval of information.

objective—a short-term step taken to reach an annual goal. Individualized education plan objectives are the steps between a student's present level of performance and an annual goal.

parallel activity—an assignment in which the outcome is similar to the outcome for other students, but the materials used to reach the outcome may be entirely different.

previewing—reading, listening to, or viewing the selection before instruction or a test.

readiness—physical, mental, and emotional preparedness for a learning activity.

receptive language—the process of receiving and understanding gestures or written or spoken language.

resource room—a setting in the school where a student receives instruction from a special education teacher for part of the school day.

Response to Intervention—a process that a school may use to identify students with specific learning disabilities. It involves universal screening for learning difficulties, providing instruction and interventions matched to the students' needs, frequent progress monitoring, and using data on students' responses to make educational decisions.

RTI—see Response to Intervention.

short attention span—inability to pay attention to something for a long period of time compared to others of the same age.

special education—specially designed instruction to meet the unique needs of a child with a disability.

special needs—a term to describe a student who has disabilities or chronic illness or is at risk for developing disabilities and who needs education services or other special services to progress.

supplemental teaching—instruction provided to the student in the form of reteaching, reinforcement, and/or alternate curriculum when needed.

supportive teaching—modifications made to the curriculum or the classroom environment by the special education teacher or paraprofessional that will allow the student to experience success in the general education setting.

sound–symbol relationship—relationship between a letter's printed form and its sound.

team teaching—two or more adults working together to develop, plan, and teach a lesson.

visual discrimination—ability to perceive likenesses and differences in pictures, words, and symbols.

References

Cicero (Version 3.05) [Computer software]. (2007). Princeton Junction, NJ: Dolphin Computer Access.

ClaroRead PLUS (Version 4.0.55) [Computer software]. (2008). Preston, UK: Claro Software.

Greene, L. J. (2002). *Winning the study game: Learning how to succeed in school.* Minnetonka, MN: Peytral.

Kurzweil 3000 (Version 10) [Computer software]. (2006). Bedford, MA: Kurzweil Educational Systems.

Scanning with Symbols 2000 (Version 2.6) [Computer software]. Cambridge, UK: Widgit Software.

Scott, V. G. (1999). *Phonemic awareness: Ready-to-use lessons, activities and games.* Minnetonka, MN: Peytral.

Scott, V. G. (2000). *Phonemic awareness: The sounds of reading* [DVD]. Minnetonka, MN. Peytral.

Stangl, K. M. (2000). *Hands-on phonics activities for elementary children.* Paramus, NJ: Center for Applied Research.

TouchMath [Computer software]. (2008). Colorado Springs, CO: Innovative Learning Concepts.

Index

CORWIN
PRESS